Christmas '13

THE BIG COOK BOOK

vegetarian

Zoe!
X
Amie

Euro
Impala
UK LIMITED

THE BIG COOK BOOK

vegetarian

© Euroimpala UK Limited

Building 3, Chiswick Park, 566 Chiswick High Road

Chiswick Town, County, London, W4 5YA

United Kingdom

Editorial production and graphic design:
Development and Creative Department

Translation: Multilingo

Printing: Printer Portugal

Legal dep.: 294483/09

How to combine vegetables

Perhaps you are one of the many people to opt for vegetarian cuisine, but maybe you don't really know where to start. You may be already familiar with it and simply want to diversify your eating habits, enjoy new recipes and vary your menu. Should you decide to start a vegetarian diet, here are some useful recommendations. The brief information given in the first few can help you to avoid getting lost among the many foods associated with this type of diet. Tofu, soya or tempeh are some examples. If you have never tried them or have doubts about them, you can learn how to prepare them and discover their best culinary applications. Rest assured that this is the Big Cook Book Vegetarian with lots of new recipes. Some are simple to do and do not need much time; others are more elaborate to be relished over longer time with family or friends. All our suggestions can refresh day to day recipes.

Vegetarianism
in harmony with Nature

Being vegetarian has become an ever more balanced way of life. Its origin goes back to Buddhism and to India's most ancient religions. However in the current Western World, justifications given by those who opt for this type of food are not religious, and are of a different nature, comprising reasons as varied as health, ethical or social issues, not forgetting humanitarian reasons.

The choice also implies an alteration in life style. Not eating meat can be a main reason for not contributing to animal exploitation in any form. As such, this is accompanied by the refusal to don woven fabrics from animals and/or consume products tested on animals – cosmetics, detergents and medicines.

Any change must be made radically and those who opt for this diet must make it a progressive habituation, so that the body gradually adapts to new food. Medical advice is recommended.

The richest and best known vegetarian diets are vegetarianism or milk-egg vegetarianism which in addition to vegetal foods, also allow the consumption of honey, dairy products and eggs. Both exclude eating any type of meat, whether it is red or white, fish or shellfish.

Followers of the vegan philosophy are lesser known. They consume foods of vegetal origin exclusively. We could refer to macrobiotics, whose food base is cereals; fruitarians who eat almost only fruit; and crudivores who only consume raw vegetable foods.

The positive aspects of the vegetarian diet are the following:

- It includes more natural, fresh and raw foods, rich in nutrients like vitamins and minerals.

- It has fewer products that are harmful to health which are not only saturated fats present in animal products, but also, sugar, sodium and refined flours.

- It provides a large amount of antioxidants, which prevent the deterioration of cells caused by free radicals.

- It provides a large quantity of fibres, which benefit intestinal transit, preventing constipation and cancer of the colon.

Nutritional
hints

Calcium needs are bypassed if you ingest dairy products daily or soya derivatives. Vitamin D, which is essential for assimilating calcium, can also be found in these as well as in butter.

■ The ingestion of foods rich in fibre should not be exaggerated, because it interferes in the absorption of nutrients.

■ Foods rich in essential fatty acids and Omega-3 such as dried fruits and vegetable oils must be included.

■ Should you opt for a diet which includes eggs, whole-grain cereals and vegetables, there is no danger of iron deficiency, since these ingredients are accompanied by foods rich in Vitamin C; a nutrient which boosts mineral absorption.

Balanced eating

SOYA – A legume very rich in high quality proteins. It has a low content of saturated fats and does not contain cholesterol. It can be stewed, cooked, sautéed or consumed raw.

Soya derivatives include:

Soya milk – Drink obtained from soya beans. It is a good alternative to cow's milk and a good source of protein. It is easily digested and does not contain cholesterol. It is sold pure or flavoured. It has a low sugar content and does not have any traces of lactose.

Soya yoghurt – It has the same consistency as normal yoghurt and is available in various flavours.

Tempeh – Fermented soya paste. It can be used as a meat

substitute. It is easily digested and is a good source of protein, fibre and Complex B Vitamins. It can be cooked, grilled or fried.

Shoyu – This is the authentic soy sauce. It can be used as a seasoning in different delicacies.

Miso – Fermented dressing produced from soya, cereals (rice or barley), salt and water. It is used for seasoning.

TOFU – Has all the essential amino acids for our bodies and supplies complete proteins. As it is rich in calcium it helps to strengthen the bones. Owing to the high content of unsaturated fatty acids, it helps to reduce cholesterol, reducing the risk of cardiac problems. It is also advised for women in menopause as it is rich in isoflavones and can alleviate the symptoms. It is easily digested and has a low calorific value.

Different types:

- Solid, it is quite versatile and can be used in almost every preparation, especially in salted dishes.

- The cream is perfect for spreading over hors d'oeuvres or adding to sauces.

- Silken tofu can be consumed raw or in soups and desserts.

Preservation and freezing:

Fresh tofu normally has a short sell by date. However UHT or dehydrated varieties already exist which are longer lasting. It is essential that it is also kept in water and in the fridge. If it floats in water, do not consume it, since this is a sign that it has decayed.

To freeze tofu, drain off the water, place it in a freezer bag and put it in the freezer. To defrost it, put it in the fridge for 14 hours before using it and then take away the excess water. It can be kept frozen for five months.

In cooking:

Tofu has little flavour; however, it absorbs flavours from other foods and condiments well during cooking. It can be used in desserts and in salted dishes (fried foods, roasts or stews.)

Agar-agar seaweed – This vegetal seaweed, originating from Japan and its seas, is an alternative to gelatine. A small tablespoonful of agar-agar is equivalent to six leaves of animal gelatine.

Nori seaweed – It is versatile and easy to prepare and can therefore be used to garnish cereals, pastries and soups. The famous sushi is made with this. To prepare it for toasts, simply place it over the flame of a cooker or an electric plate until it becomes crunchy and has a pleasant smell. This seaweed is rich in Vitamins A, B1, B2, PP, B6, B12, C and folic acid.

Seitan – This is an excellent meat substitute with similar appearance, firmness, texture and flavour. Produced from wheat flour, it is a food which is very rich in proteins, fibre and minerals.

Bulgur – This is produced from different types of wheat grains which are partially cooked then normally dried in the sun and then separated. It is frequently used in oriental cooking and is a basic element of Turkish cuisine.

Vegetarian sausages and hamburgers – are also products which can be produced from soya or seitan and can contain mixes of seaweed and mushrooms.

RECIPES

INGREDIENTS

1 cucumber
2 tomatoes
1/2 red pepper
1/2 green pepper
2 cloves garlic
100 g bread
50 ml olive oil
salt, pepper, croutons
and coriander to taste

Easy

30 minutes

4

Gaspacho

Wash all vegetables and chop them into pieces or cubes. Keep a little aside to garnish and grind the rest.

Take a crust of bread; cut it into pieces and add it to the previous preparation along with the olive oil. Continue to crush it.

Add water to taste until the desired consistency is obtained. Serve the fresh *gaspacho* with vegetables kept aside, croutons and small leaves of coriander.

Carrot soup

Peel the carrots, pumpkin, potatoes, onions and garlic cloves. Wash all of these vegetables, cut them into chunks and cook them in salted water.

Wash the leek in cold water and also cut it into medium-sized pieces, adding the remaining vegetables only when they are cooked.

Take away from the heat, grinding everything and leave until the soup is completely cooled.

Then put it into the fridge until it becomes very cool. When serving make the soup velvety with fresh cream and adjust to taste.

INGREDIENTS

250 g carrot
100 g pumpkin
300 g potatoes
2 onions
2 cloves garlic
1.2 l water
100 g leek
2 dl cream
salt to taste

2 cucumbers
400 g potatoes
2 onions
100 g leek
1.2 l water
1 natural yoghurt
salt to taste

Cucumber soup

Easy //

30 minutes

4

Cut one of the cucumbers into four sections; set aside. Peel the potatoes, onions and the remaining cucumber. Wash all vegetables as well as the leek and cut them into pieces.

Cook them in salted water over a gentle heat. When everything has been cooked, take the soup off the heat and blend it. Adjust the seasoning and keep it in the fridge until it becomes very cold.

Transfer the yoghurt to a bowl and mix well with a fork. Mix the cream in and serve, garnishing with the reserved cucumber rounds.

Soya beansprout soup

Wash the soya beansprouts and set aside. Peel the potatoes, carrots and the pumpkin. Cook them in water. Add the cumin and season with salt.

Add the cubed onions, the diced leek and cloves of garlic. Leave to simmer over a gentle heat. Grind and adjust the seasoning. Serve the soup with the soya beansprouts and spring onion.

INGREDIENTS

100 g soya beansprouts
400 g potatoes
200 g carrots
100 g pumpkin
1.2 l water
a pinch cumin
2 onions
100 g leeks
2 cloves garlic
1 tablespoon chopped spring onion
salt to taste

INGREDIENTS

100 g leeks
1.2 l water
1 tablespoon miso
100 g runner beans
80 g hakubaku somen
(Japanese noodles)
salt to taste

Miso and runner bean broth

Easy
20 minutes
4

Cut the leek into large strips and leave them to one side. Heat up the water seasoned with salt and when it has reached boiling point add the miso and blend until it is dissolved.

Add the strips of leek, the runner beans, cut into pieces, and the hakubaku somen noodles. When everything is cooked, remove from the heat and serve immediately.

Miso and wakame soup

Heat the water with the wakame and bring to the boil. Add the vegetables and leave them to cook until they become soft.

Dissolve the miso in a little of the broth and season the soup with it. Leave to cook for three minutes without boiling and serve with chopped spring onion and grated ginger.

INGREDIENTS

2 l water
1 strip of wakame
1 onion sliced into
  half moons
1 sliced carrot
1 sliced turnip
2 tablespoons miso
chopped spring onion
and grated ginger
to taste

INGREDIENTS

10 g kombu seaweed
1.2 l water
150 g turnip
150 g pumpkin
150 g green beans
150 g mushrooms
2 tablespoons miso
salt to taste

SUGGESTION

Add a few peas
to the vegetables
used and 30 grams
of hiziki seaweed.

Easy

35 minutes

4

Miso and kombu seaweed soup

Immerse the seaweed into the water, until returns to its original state. Prepare the vegetables and the mushrooms, cutting them into pieces. Then heat the first preparation and season with salt.

When it has started to boil, add the vegetables and the mushrooms and leave to cook for 15 minutes. Remove from the heat, mix in the miso and serve.

Seaweed soup

Soak the wakame seaweed in hot water for 20 minutes. Then boil the water with the tofu, cut into small cubes, and the soaked wakame seaweed.

Add the vermicelli, cut into pieces, and leave to cook for five minutes. Mix in the miso paste serve with a sprinkling of chopped coriander.

INGREDIENTS

1 sheet of wakame
seaweed
1.5 l water
100 g tofu
100 g vermicelli
1 teaspoon miso
1 sprig coriander
salt and pepper to taste

SUGGESTION
Also add a quarter of
a sheet of nori seaweed.

INGREDIENTS

50 ml olive oil
300 g carrots
1 small onion
2 cloves garlic
1.5 l water
100 g peas
200 g cauliflower
60 g vermicelli
1 level tablespoon miso
salt to taste

SUGGESTION
Sprinkle the soup with
small cubes of tofu.

Miso with vermicelli

Easy
30 minutes
4

Sauté the carrots in olive oil with the onion and cloves of garlic all cut into small pieces. Leave to settle and season with salt.

Cover with water and leave to cook for 10 minutes. Add the peas, cauliflower in small florets and the vermicelli. Leave to cook and mix in the miso. When it has reached boiling point, remove from heat and serve.

Cream
of fresh mushroom

Cook the mushrooms, cut into quarters, in olive oil. Remove them and set aside. Brown the potatoes and chopped carrot in the same oil and add the maize.

Add water and season with salt and pepper. Leave to cook until the vegetables become soft. Reduce the soup to a purée and serve the cream with the mushrooms.

INGREDIENTS

200 g fresh white
mushrooms
5 tablespoons olive oil
600 g potatoes
1 carrot
200 g sweet maize
1.2 l water
salt and pepper to taste

1 watercress sauce
1 small onion
1 clove garlic
400 g potatoes
200 g carrots
1 courgette
50 ml olive oil
1.5 l water
1 tablespoon soya sauce
salt and pepper to taste

Cream of vegetables

Easy

35 minutes

4

Prepare the watercress and cut the remaining vegetables into chunks, except for a quarter of the carrots. Sauté them all in olive oil. Add water and leave to cook. Remove and blend the soup.

Cut the reserved peeled carrots into strips and add the soup. Leave to cook and finally add the soya sauce. Serve immediately.

ENTRÉES AND SOUPS

Cream of leek

Cut the leek into rounds. Wash them and cook them in water, seasoned with salt. Peel the onion, carrots, shaya root and the garlic. Cut them all into pieces. Remove the cooked leek from the heat and reserve.

Cook the chopped vegetables in the same water, as well as the peeled and seeded tomatoes. Add the olive oil and leave to simmer for 10 minutes over a gentle heat. Remove from the heat and blend well. Season and add the reserved leek. Garnish with spring onion and serve.

INGREDIENTS

100 g leeks
1.2 l water
1 onion
2 carrots
1 shaya root
2 cloves garlic
500 g ripe tomatoes
2 tablespoons olive oil
1 tablespoon
spring onions
salt to taste

SUGGESTION
Add two tablespoons
of cooking soya
before blending.

INGREDIENTS

200 g leeks
200 g potatoes
1 onion
350 g cauliflower
1 clove garlic
1 l water
1 dl soya milk
salt, flour and oil
to taste

SUGGESTION
Substitute the soya
milk with skimmed
natural yoghurt

Cauliflower soup

Easy
25 minutes
4

Wash the leek and cut the green part à la julienne. Dredge it in flour and fry it in oil. Drain it on absorbent paper and reserve.

Peel the potatoes and the onion and cut them into pieces, together with the cauliflower, the remaining leek and the garlic.

Leave everything to simmer in water seasoned with salt over a gentle heat. Then blend well and adjust the seasoning. Smoothen with the soya milk and serve the soup with the reserved strips of leek.

Spinach bread

Blanch the spinach in salted boiling water, drain it and reserve. Dissolve the yeast in lukewarm water. Mix the flour with the yeast preparation separately and gradually. Mix well until a ball of dough is formed. Add salt and knead again. Leave to rise for 30 minutes.

Roll the dough out over a floured surface and stuff with spinach. Then roll it up and place on a tray. Leave to rise for approximately 30 minutes. Place in an oven set at 200° C for 40 minutes. Remove, leave to rest, then serve the bread cut into thin slices.

INGREDIENTS

200 g frozen spinach
30 g baking yeast
2 dl water
300 g flour
100 g soya flour
1 tablespoon salt
flour and salt to taste

SUGGESTION
Use a mould to make several layers of spinach and dough.

INGREDIENTS

4 carrots
4 stalks celery with
foliage
1 endive
8 radishes
curly lettuce leaves
mayonnaise, cocktail
sauce, tartar sauce
and yoghurt to taste

Saucy vegetables

Easy

10 minutes

4

Peel the carrots, cut them into sticks and place them in cold water along with some lettuce leaves. Cut the celery into strips, the endive full length and the radishes into quarters. Drain the vegetables and place them in a serving dish. Accompany with various sauces.

Mayonnaise – Place three egg yolks in a bowl, salt and pepper to taste, a teaspoon of mustard, a few drops of vinegar and begin to beat with a whisk. When well beaten and still continuing to stir, add four decilitres of olive oil in trickles. Finally mix in a tablespoon of vinegar.

Cocktail sauce – Mix together a decilitre of mayonnaise, three tablespoons of ketchup and a little brandy. Season with salt and pepper. Serve garnished with spring onion.

Tartar sauce – Mix a decilitre of mayonnaise with a tablespoon of chopped pickles and also a chopped boiled egg. Season with salt and pepper.

Yoghurt sauce – Mix natural yoghurt with two tablespoonfuls of cream cheese and a tablespoonful of chopped aromatic herbs. Season with salt and pepper.

Vegetable paté

Tofu and herb paté – Mix 200 grams of soft tofu with a sprig of parsley, a sprig of rosemary, coriander, thyme, pennyroyal, a teaspoon of mustard, a clove of garlic and a small onion in a blender with the last two items chopped. Blend everything and add a little olive oil to obtain the desired consistency. Season with salt and pepper and serve the paté garnished with thyme.

Aubergine and mushroom paté – Chop 400 grams of mushrooms, 200 grams of peeled aubergines, a small onion and two cloves of garlic. Sauté them in a decilitre of olive oil. Season with salt and pepper and leave to cook until they are all tender. Remove and leave to cool. Then cool and grind the paté.

Seed and almond paté – Crush three tablespoons of linseed with two tablespoonfuls of hemp seeds with a pestle and mortar. When they begin to break up, add two tablespoons of shelled almond sauce, two tablespoons of olive oil and season with salt and pepper. Continue to grind until a paste is obtained. When everything has broken up, grind the preparation until a more homogenous paste is obtained.

INGREDIENTS

1 tofu and herbs
paté recipe
1 aubergine and
mushroom paté recipe
1 seed and almond
paté recipe

For accompaniment:
1 packet breadsticks
1 packet toast slices
1 pack of biscuits

4 ripe tomatoes
4 buffalo mozzarella
4 nori seaweed leaves
fresh coriander, soya
sauce and wasabia
to taste

Vegetarian sushi

Easy

15 minutes

4

Blanch the tomato in boiling water. Skin it, remove its seeds, cut it into sections and reserve. Cut each of the buffalo mozzarella cheeses into four parts.

Lay out the nori seaweed leaves in lines for sushi. Layer the tomato sections and one of the pieces of mozzarella on each line of seaweed. Roll up, applying pressure and leave the sushi rolls to cool for a few minutes. Before serving, cut each roll into four,

garnish with fresh coriander and accompany with soya sauce and wasabia.

Soya sauce and wasabia – If the wasabia is in powder form, prepare it 30 minutes beforehand by gradually mixing a tablespoon of this powder with water until the consistency of a paste is obtained. Knead it into a ball and cover it with cling film. Leave to rest for the time indicated above.

Avocado pear tartare

Peel the avocado pears and cut them into small cubes. Season with salt, pepper and lemon juice. Cut the tomato, skin and seed it and cut it in the same way. Coarsely chop part of the spring onion. Add these two ingredients then sprinkle with liqueur. Leave to flavour for a few minutes.

Using small rings, mould the avocado pear preparation onto serving dishes. Carefully remove the rings and garnish with half of the radishes, cut into fine rounds, and the rest of the spring onion in small pieces and the remaining radishes cut finely à la julienne. Serve immediately.

INGREDIENTS

2 avocado pears
2 lemons (juice)
150 g plum tomatoes
1 sprig of spring onion
1 teaspoon of liqueur
to taste
100 g radishes
salt and pepper to taste

INGREDIENTS

2 carrots
2 courgettes
2 stalks of celery
with foliage
400 g fresh puff pastry
1 tin soya shoots
flour to taste
1 beaten egg

Sauce:
1 natural yoghurt
1 lemon (juice)
1 sprig of mint
salt and pepper to taste

Vegetarian roll

Easy

1 hour

6

Cut the carrots, courgettes and celery into fine strips. Blanch in plenty of boiling water, drain and leave to one side. Turn the oven on at 180° C. Roll the puff pastry out over a floured surface and scatter the soya beansprouts over it. Season with salt and pepper and roll up.

Place the roll on a baking tray; coat it with beaten egg and leave in the oven for 20 minutes. To prepare the sauce: Mix the yoghurt with the lemon juice and chopped mint. Season with salt and pepper and cover. Serve the vegetarian roll garnished as required and accompany with the sauce served separately.

Seitan mille-feuilles and sweet potato

Grease small moulds smoothly with soya margarine and keep to one side. Peel the potatoes, cut them into rounds and blanch in boiling water. Drain them, keeping the boiling water aside and cool with a little ice.

Slice the carrots and blanch them in the reserved water. Remove them and reserve them together with the potatoes. Cut the seitan into slices. Switch the oven on at 180° C.

Place alternate layers of potatoes, carrots and slices of seitan into the moulds. Mix the eggs with the cream, season with salt, pepper and nutmeg. Pour into the moulds and place in centre of the oven for 15 minutes. Remove, take out of the moulds and garnish with dill.

INGREDIENTS

4 large sweet potatoes
2 carrots
2 packs seitan
3 eggs
2 dl soya margarine
cream, salt, pepper,
nutmeg and dill to taste

2 avocado-pears
1/2 lemon (juice)
2 ripe tomatoes
1 tablespoon
Worcestershire sauce
1 teaspoon soya sauce
1 teaspoon Tabasco
1 clove garlic
1 sprig coriander
1 pack salted maize chips
salt and pepper to taste

Guacamole

Average //
15 minutes
4

Peel the avocado-pears and place them in a bowl. Crush them with a fork and add lemon juice to prevent the pulp darkening. Wash and cut the tomatoes into small cubes. Remove the skin and seeds.

Add them to the avocado-pears and mix well with the Worcestershire sauce, soya sauce, Tabasco and the finally chopped glove of garlic. Season with salt and pepper. Finely cut the coriander and also add it to the avocado-pear preparation. Serve with maize chips.

Vegetarian tortillas

Peel the courgette and cut it very finely à la julienne as well as the white part of the leek. Sauté in olive oil. Add the maize and season with salt and pepper. Remove and set aside.

Blanch the foliage of the leek in cold water, remove and cut it into strips. Cut the tomato into half moons and set aside. Beat the yoghurt and mayonnaise mixture in a container with a whisk.

Season with salt and pepper and add mint chopped à la julienne.

Heat the tortillas in a frying pan. Put the filling in the centre together with the tomato, roll and tie with the blanched strips of leek. Serve with the sauce immediately.

INGREDIENTS

1 courgette
1 leek with foliage
1 tablespoon olive oil
1 tin sweet maize
3 plum tomatoes
1 natural yoghurt
1 tablespoon mayonnaise
1 sprig mint
1 packet Mexican tortillas
salt and pepper to taste

SUGGESTION
Add a small tin of drained haricot beans.

INGREDIENTS

30 g baking yeast
1 kg flour
100 g broccoli
1/2 turnip
150 g carrots
80 g soya shoots
150 g green beans
1 dl olive oil
1 onion
2 cloves garlic
1 egg yolk
salt, pepper and flour
to taste

Stuffed bread

Easy //
1 hour
8

Dissolve the baking yeast into a little water. Then mix with the flour and knead them together with a little water.
Then leave the kneaded dough to rise for two hours at room temperature.

Prepare the vegetables and cut them into pieces. Blanch them separately in plenty of boiling water, seasoned with salt, pepper and half of olive oil. Chop and sauté the onion and the cloves of garlic in the remaining olive oil. Mix the vegetables in and leave to sauté for a few minutes. Set the oven at 180° C.

Roll the dough out over a floured surface, stuff it with the vegetables and roll it. Brush the top with the beaten egg yolk and put in the oven for 40 minutes. Remove and serve warm or lukewarm.

Vegetable crepes

Peel the onion, cut it into half moons and sauté in butter. Cut the vegetables à la julienne, wash them in cold water and add them to the sauce. Sauté them well and mix in the soya sauce. Season with salt and remove from the heat.

Distribute the preparation in each of the crepe sheets and roll carefully so that the filling does not come out. Cover the crepes with the beaten egg, breadcrumbs and fry them in plenty of warm oil.

INGREDIENTS

1 onion
2 tablespoons butter
100 g savoy cabbage
1 carrot
50 g soya beansprouts
100 g leek
2 mushrooms
1 cofeespoon soya sauce
4 crepes
2 eggs
salt, breadcrumbs
and oil to taste

SUGGESTION

When removing the sautéed vegetables from the heat, add strips of cheese. Roll the crepes and fry them.

INGREDIENTS

2 large crepes
80 g Spanish peppers
300 g sushi rice
3 tablespoons mirin
(Japanese drink)
3 leaves nori seaweed
1 teaspoon horseradish
paste
salt, pepper and soya
sauce to taste

Egg and pepper sushi

Easy //
35 minutes
4

Cut the crepes into small slices, cut the peppers and set aside. Cook the rice following the instructions on the packet and leave to cool. Mix the mirin in.

Arrange the seaweed over a surface and place the rice on top of it. Place one layer of crepes and another layer of the peppers onto the rice. Roll tightly and cut into rounds. Serve with soya sauce and horseradish paste.

Soya and curry pies

Grease the small tart baking moulds with butter and set aside. Chop the onion, cloves of garlic and heat in olive oil along with the soya. Peel the turnip and chop it up with the tomato. Mix into the mixture and season with curry and paprika.

Add the grated carrot and leave to cook, adding the white wine. After it has soaked in, sprinkle with chopped parsley, remove and set aside.

Roll the puff pastry out on a floured surface and line the moulds with it. Fill them with the soya preparation and cover them with the puff pastry to form lids. Place the pies on a tray and put in the oven, set at 180° C, for approximately 20 minutes. Remove and serve hot or cold.

INGREDIENTS

1 small onion
2 cloves garlic
50 ml olive oil
100 g fine textured soya
50 g turnip
80 g peeled tomato
1 tablespoon curry powder
1 teaspoon paprika
50 g carrots
1 dl white wine
400 g puff pastry
butter, flour and parsley to taste

Easy

30 minutes

4

Vegetable tofu cornucopia

Cut the vegetables into pieces, blanch them separately in plenty of water, seasoned with salt and pepper to taste, drain them and set aside.

Cut the tofu into small cubes and put in a frying pan with the olive oil and almonds. Leave them to fry until they are really browned and add the vegetables. Add the soya sauce and a little water and season with thyme.

Leave to boil continuously stirring, remove from the heat and leave to cool. Put the mixture on top of the crepes and roll them into a cone. Then serve them immediately.

Soya pastries

Soak the soya beans for an hour. Grind them and place them in a bowl under running water to remove the skins. Drain and grind again with the peeled onion, cut into pieces and the chopped coriander.

Season with salt and pepper to taste. Mould into small pastries using two tablespoons, making them a bit like cod balls and fry them in hot oil. Drain them on absorbent paper and serve with a little green salad.

INGREDIENTS

350 g soya beans
1 medium-sized onion
1 tablespoon freshly chopped coriander
salt, pepper, oil and lettuce to taste

SUGGESTION
Substitute the soya beans with cowpeas.

INGREDIENTS

100 g oats
1 sprig thyme
300 g green beans
300 g carrots
100 g peas
50 ml olive oil
3 cloves
of chopped garlic
salt and pepper to taste

SUGGESTION
Mix a tablespoon of
soya and balsamic vinegar
to season the vegetables.

Vegetable salad
with oats

Easy
30 minutes
4

Cook the oats in plenty of water and season with salt and pepper and a sprig of thyme. Remove from the heat, drain them, leave to cool and keep in the fridge.

Then cook the vegetables, cut into pieces, in plenty of water, seasoned with salt and pepper. Mix everything and season with olive oil, chopped garlic and salt and pepper.

Vegetable pie

Mix the eggs, flour, salt and the yeast well. Add water, olive oil and knead until the preparation is mouldable. Grease a flan dish with butter. Roll the pastry out, cut out a large circle the size of the flan dish and set aside. Line the flan dish with the remaining pastry.

Cook the cauliflower and beans in salted water. Remove them and chop them, the aubergine, pepper, onion and cloves of garlic.

Mix everything with the spices. Season with salt and pepper and fold in some grated cheese.

Pour this preparation onto the pastry in the flan dish and cover with the circle of pastry set aside. Press the edges together applying a little pressure so that the pie is tightly sealed. Brush with beaten egg yolk and put in the oven, set at 190º C, for 20 minutes. Remove and serve.

INGREDIENTS

2 eggs
300 g wheat flour
1 teaspoon yeast power
1 dl water
50 ml olive oil
100 g cauliflower
200 g green beans
1/2 aubergine
1/2 red pepper
1 small onion
3 cloves garlic
1 teaspoon coriander seeds
1 teaspoon piri-piri
1 teaspoon cardamom
1 teaspoon curry
50 g grated cheese
1 egg yolk
salt, pepper and butter to taste

INGREDIENTS

5 ripe tomatoes
2 dl water
1 sprig thyme
100 g couscous
1 chopped onion
30 ml olive oil
1 chopped sprig coriander
salt and pepper to taste

Easy
30 minutes
4

Couscous
stuffed tomatoes

Cut the tops off four tomatoes and with a spoon remove the pulp and the seeds. Heat the water, seasoned with salt, pepper and thyme. Cut the remaining tomato into cubes and mix with the couscous.

Add the onion, mix with the olive oil and season with salt and pepper to taste. Add boiling water to the couscous and leave to dry. Mix it with the coriander and stuff the tomatoes with this preparation. Garnish to taste and serve.

Pumpkin with tapioca

Peel the pumpkin and cut into pieces. Wash it and arrange on a baking tray. Season with salt and pepper and add water and olive oil. Place in the middle of the oven set at 180° C for 25 minutes.

Soak the tapioca in cold water for 10 minutes. When the pumpkin has been cooking for 10 minutes add the tapioca and sprinkle with honey. Remove and serve with sesame seeds.

INGREDIENTS

1.2 kg pumpkin
1 dl olive oil
70 g tapioca
3 tablespoons honey
1 teaspoon
sesame seeds
salt and pepper to taste

SUGGESTION
Add a teaspoon of ginger
to the pumpkin.

INGREDIENTS

250 g baby carrots
1 bunch green asparagus
400 g Brussels sprouts
200 ml béchamel sauce
salt and butter to taste

COOKING
SUGGESTION
Add 100 g mushrooms
cut in half to
vegetables.

Vegetables with béchamel

Easy
30 minutes
4

Cook baby carrots in water and season with salt. Drain and sauté in butter. Arrange asparagus and cook in boiling water, season with salt Brussels sprouts.

Mix vegetables, place in a heat resistant container and pour with béchamel sauce. Put at the top of the oven to cook au gratin. Remove and serve immediately.

ENTRÉES AND SOUPS

Vegetable bread

Mix flour, eggs and diluted baking powder with water, until a homogenous dough. Place in a warm and dry place for two hours. Turn on the oven at 80° C.

Cook asparagus in plenty of water for 10 minutes. Remove, drain and cut into pieces like the artichoke hearts. Place on a tray with olives and bake for 20 minutes. Brush a mould with butter and powder with flour.

Mix vegetables into the dough and make small balls. Put in the mould and brush with corn jelly. Sprinkle with seeds and rosemary leaves. Bake at 200° C, for 30 minutes. Remove and leave cool before serving.

INGREDIENTS

400 g flour
2 eggs
12 g baking powder
100 ml water
1 bunch green asparagus
1 tin artichoke hearts
3 tablespoons black
olives
2 tablespoons corn jelly
1 tablespoon coriander
seeds
1 tablespoon poppy seeds
1 rosemary sprig
butter and flour to
taste

INGREDIENTS

200 g bar flamengo
cheese
2 pears
200 g artichoke bulbs
2 tomatoes
1 lemon (juice)
2 garlic cloves
1 tablespoon pine nuts
1 tablespoon grated
Parmesan cheese
1 sprig basil
100 ml olive oil
1 tablespoon hemp seeds
salt, pepper and lettuce
to taste

SUGGESTION

Add walnuts and raisins
to salad.

Easy

20 minutes

4

Exotic salad with pesto

Cut flamengo cheese into cubes, pears into small pieces, artichoke bulbs into triangles and the tomato into small cubes, without seeds. Mix everything and sprinkle with lemon juice.

In a pestle, grind the garlic cloves, pine nuts, Parmesan cheese and basil into a paste. Dissolve in the olive oil and mix well. Season with salt and pepper and dress the salad and lettuce. Sprinkle with hemp seeds.

Endives with olives and cheese

Remove larger leaves from endives and set aside. Wash and cut tomato, onion and cheese into small cubes.

Mix all with oregano, olive oil and vinegar. Season with salt and pepper; fill endive leaves with this mixture and serve.

INGREDIENTS

2 endives
1 large tomato
1 small onion
100 g cheese
1 teaspoon oregano
50 ml olive oil
1 tablespoon vinegar
salt and pepper to taste

SUGGESTION

Season with thyme and chopped pennyroyals (mint).

INGREDIENTS

Dough:
250 g flour
125 g butter
100 ml water
flour to powder
vegetable butter
to grease

Filling:
100 g broccoli
2 tomatoes
2 medium sized onions
1/2 leek
50 ml olive oil
3 eggs
300 ml milk
80 g grated flamengo
cheese
salt, pepper
and nutmeg to taste

Vegetable quiche

Easy
40 minutes
4

Prepare the dough, mixing all ingredients. Roll over a floured surface and line a pie plate, previously greased with vegetable butter; set aside.

Make the filling: Cut the broccoli into pieces and scald in boiling water for five minutes; set aside. Cut the tomato into cubes, and the onions and leeks into rounds. Stew the last two ingredients in olive oil, let cook a little; set aside.

Separately, beat the eggs with the milk. Place the stew in pie dish and arrange tomato and broccoli on top. Season with salt, pepper and nutmeg. Cover with egg mixture and sprinkle with grated cheese. Bake at 170° C for 40 minutes.

whole rice fritters

Cook rice in salted water for 20 minutes. Transfer to a container; add breadcrumbs and eggs. Adjust the seasoning and make little balls.

Coat with beaten egg and breadcrumbs, heat the oil and fry. Drain excess fat in paper towel. Garnish rice fritters with small leaves of parsley and serve.

INGREDIENTS

300 g whole rice
700 ml water
2 tablespoons breadcrumbs
2 eggs
1 sprig parsley
beaten egg, breadcrumbs and oil to taste

SUGGESTION

Stuff fritters with stoned black olives.

INGREDIENTS

250 g sushi rice
500 ml water
1/2 red pepper
1 medium carrot
1 medium courgette
6 leaves of nori seaweed
salt and vinegar to taste

SUGGESTION
Put a little water
with vinegar on
a plate and moisten
hands to work the
rice due to its viscosity.

Courgette and pepper sushi

Average
1 hour
4

Rinse the rice a few times in water, until it becomes completely clean. Then, cook in hot water, seasoned with salt; let cook for 15 minutes.

Cut the pepper, carrot and courgette into small slices, cook in salt water and set aside.

After rice is cooked, place in a pan and mix frequently to cool. Make a mixture of three tablespoons of vinegar to one of water.

Pour over the rice and stir well.

When rice is cold, put a portion on a seaweed leaf; arrange sliced and cooked vegetables on top. Roll, applying a little pressure. Serve garnished to taste.

Little tofu bags
with vegetables

Soak little bags of tofu in water for 20 minutes. Separate endive leaves and cut in strips. Remove tomato skin and seeds and slice into small chunks. Sautee in half the butter; season with salt and pepper and set aside.

Heat remaining butter and, as soon as melted, add bread-crumbs. Mix gently and gradually add soy milk. Mix in two egg yolks and let cook a little. Add mixture to reserved endives and let cook a little more; set aside.

Drain, open and fill little bags with previous mixture. Refrigerate for 10 minutes. Then, coat with the remaining beaten egg and corn flour mixed with sesame. Fry the little bags in plenty of oil and drain on paper towel. Serve with mixed salad.

INGREDIENTS

8 little bags tofu
2 endives
2 ripe tomatoes
50 g butter
4 tablespoons
breadcrumbs
350 ml soy milk
3 eggs
1 tablespoon sesame
corn flour, salt, pepper,
sunflower oil
and mixed salad to taste

4 medium aubergines
1 onion
1 clove garlic
3 tablespoons
butter
150 g leek
2 chilli peppers
6 mushrooms
1 tablespoon tomato pulp
2 tablespoons Port wine
salt, pepper, coriander
in grains, cumin
and spring onion to taste

Oriental aubergine

Average
40 minutes
4

Cut off the top and bottom of each aubergine. Remove the pulp without damaging the skin; set aside. Chop the onion, garlic clove and stew in butter. Add leek rounds and chilli pepper. Season with salt and pepper; add mushrooms, cut into pieces and let sauté.

Add tomato pulp and Port wine. Season with coriander grains and cumin; mix and add the aubergine pulp. Stew the aubergines with this preparation and bake in the oven for 15 minutes. Remove and serve with spring onion.

Oat and mushroom croquettes

Easy
30 minutes
4

Stew the onion and garlic cloves, both chopped, in olive oil. Allow to gain colour and add mushrooms, also chopped. Season with salt and pepper and then mix in oat flakes well.

As soon as they begin to dry, cover with water. Let cook slowly until the water evaporates. Let cool and make croquettes. Coat in flour and fry in hot oil. Serve the croquettes on a bed of lettuce.

INGREDIENTS

1 small onion
2 cloves garlic
50 ml olive oil
200 g white mushrooms
200 g button mushrooms
200 g oat flakes
salt, pepper, water,
flour, oil
and lettuce to taste

SUGGESTION
Add two chopped artichoke bulbs.

Easy //

30 minutes

4

Baby potatoes in tomato

Peel potatoes and boil in salted water; cut into average sized pieces and set aside. Chop garlic and onion and stew in olive oil. Add the chopped ripe tomato, flour, sugar and chopped aromatic herbs.

Season with salt and pepper and let sit a little, mixing continuously. Pour in boiling water and cook on low heat until thickened. Then strain, place potatoes in the sauce and let boil and serve.

Focaccia with oregano

Grease a rectangular mould with butter. Prepare dough, mixing the flour with the salt. Dissolve the bakers yeast in a little water and mix with flour. Add more water, if necessary, to form a soft and mouldable dough.

Cover and let rise for one hour. Place in the mould, brush with olive oil and powder with oregano. Bake at 220° C, for 15 minutes. Remove, take the focaccia out of the mould and serve immediately.

INGREDIENTS

750 g flour
1 tablespoon fine salt
20 g baker yeast
100 ml olive oil
butter to grease
oregano to taste

SUGGESTION
Mix into dough four tablespoons olives, without stones and in small rings.

INGREDIENTS

250 g tofu
2 ripe tomatoes
2 teaspoons capers
50 ml olive oil
1/2 lemon (juice)
1 teaspoon vinegar
coarse salt and mixed
lettuce to taste

SUGGESTION
Add a teaspoon coriander
seeds into the mortar.

Tofu carpaccio

Easy
30 minutes
4

Cut the tofu into fine sheets and tomato into rounds. Crush a little coarse salt in a mortar with the capers, olive oil, lemon juice and vinegar.

Season the tofu with this mixture; let marinate for two hours. Drain and serve tofu carpaccio with tomato rounds and some lettuce leaves. Sprinkle with sauce.

Broccoli
meat balls

Arrange the broccoli and cook in salted water; drain and set aside. Peel and cook potatoes. Smash with a fork, as well as the broccoli and set aside.

Chop the onion and garlic cloves; peel carrot, cut into half moons and stew all in olive oil. Add chopped tomato, a pinch of sugar and the aromatic herbs.

Season with salt and pepper and let sit a little, stirring frequently. Add water and cook on low heat, until thickened, set aside.

Make small balls with mashed potato and broccoli; coat with beaten egg and breadcrumbs. Fry in plenty of oil and drain on paper towel. Serve accompanied by remaining sauce.

INGREDIENTS

250 g broccoli
450 g potatoes
1 onion
3 cloves garlic
1 small carrot
50 ml olive oil
1 large tin peeled
tomatoes
1 sprig varied aromatic
herbs
150 ml boiling water
3 eggs
150 g breadcrumbs
salt, sugar, oil
and pepper to taste

INGREDIENTS

1 onion
3 cloves garlic
50 ml olive oil
300 g rice
1/2 red pepper
1 carrot
100 g broccoli
650 ml hot water
2 tablespoons
chopped olives
salt, oil, mayonnaise
and spring onion to taste

SUGGESTION
Add two tablespoons
chopped cashew nuts
to the rice when adding
the olives.

Easy //

40 minutes

4

Rice hamburger with vegetables

Turn on the oven at 180° C. Peel and chop the onion and garlic cloves and stew in olive oil. Add the rice, pepper, carrot and broccoli cut into small pieces. Add the water, season with salt and cook on a low heat for 12 minutes.

Remove from heat and add the olives. Let cool and make the hamburgers. Place on a tray, previously greased with a little oil and bake in the oven for 10 minutes. Remove and serve with a little mayonnaise on each hamburger, sprinkled with chopped spring onion.

Vegetable and oat fingers

Soak oats for 15 minutes. Peel and chop the onion and garlic cloves and stew in olive oil. Peel the aubergine; also chop and add to mixture. Season with salt, and pepper and let stew a little. Drain oats; reserve water and add the cereal to the mixture, stirring well. Add the remaining water until the ingredients are covered.

Aside, cook broccoli and cauliflower separately. Remove and chop. Add to previous preparation and leave to cook until swollen. Remove from heat, and after cooling, cut into rectangles. Sieve flour over the fingers, beaten egg and breadcrumbs. Fry in very hot oil and serve immediately, garnished to taste.

INGREDIENTS

150 g fine oats
1 small onion
3 cloves garlic
50 ml olive oil
1/2 aubergine
300 g broccoli
200 g cauliflower
3 eggs
salt, pepper,
breadcrumbs, flour
and oil to taste

SUGGESTION
Add a teaspoon of grated ginger to stew.

INGREDIENTS

Dough:
200 g flour
100 g vegetable margarine
salt to taste

Filling:
150 g carrots
100 g peas
150 g okra
3 eggs
200 ml milk
salt, pepper, flour
and butter to taste

SUGGESTION
Add a teaspoon of
freshly chopped
oregano to vegetables.

Vegetable mini-quiche

Easy
50 minutes
4

Prepare the dough, mixing the flour well with a pinch of salt, the margarine and a little water until a homogenous dough is obtained. Then, let sit in the fridge, for 15 minutes. Switch on the oven at 180° C.

Make filling: Wash, peel and cut carrots into small cubes. Cook in boiling water with peas and okra, washed and cut into fine rounds. Aside, beat the eggs with cold milk and season with a little salt and pepper.

Roli dough on a floured surface and line small quiche moulds, greased with butter and sprinkled with flour. Fill with the cooked vegetables and with the milk and egg mixture. Bake quiches in the oven for 20 minutes. Remove and serve.

Tofu rice and vegetables

Heat a pan with olive oil, chopped garlic cloves, laurel and chopped onion. Add rice and fry; season with salt and pepper. Add the boiling water and let cook gently for 10 minutes.

Cook, in water seasoned with salt, the red and green peppers, washed and cut into cubes, baby courgettes cut diagonally, pumpkin in cubes, asparagus and baby corn. Drain vegetables and keep in a cool place.

Five minutes after cooking the rice, add the cooked vegetables, with Greek tofu, cut into cubes, and the drained red beans. Mix and let cook. Serve hot, garnished with a sprig of thyme.

INGREDIENTS

50 ml olive oil
2 cloves garlic
1 laurel leaf
1 onion
300 g rice
600 ml water
1/2 green pepper
1/2 red pepper
3 baby courgettes
200 g pumpkin
12 small green asparagus
8 baby corn ears
200 g Greek tofu
1/2 tin red beans
1 sprig thyme
salt and pepper to taste

INGREDIENTS

1 small turnip
4 green apples
1/2 lemon (juice)
300 ml mayonnaise
100 ml cream
100 g walnut
1 lettuce root
1/2 packet arugula
fine salt and pepper
to taste

Stuffed apples

Medium
35 minutes
4

Peel turnip and cut into strips; season with salt, pepper, and leave to flavour for 20 minutes. Wash apples and remove tops, like a lid. Make small slashes in the skin; remove the pulp without damaging the skin and sprinkle the insides with lemon juice.

Cut remaining pulp into strips and mix well with mayonnaise; add cream and season with salt and pepper to taste. Add turnip strips and mix delicately, in such a way as to mix all ingredients well.

Reserve a quarter of the filling and fill the rest into the apples. Decorate with some nuts; put the apple lids back on top, add a little of the reserved filling. Wash and place salad and arrange around apples. Garnish with the remaining chopped walnut.

Crunchy strips

Combine flour, with vinegar and oil in mixing bowl, and mix very well. Add the water and a pinch of salt. Knead until a soft mixture is obtained. Let rest for 15 minutes.

Roll dough on a floured surface to a fine thickness. With a dough cutter, cut into various rectangles, not very large; make a small slit in the centre of each one.

Fry the rectangles in plenty of hot oil. Then, remove and let drain on paper towel. Place crunchy strips in a bowl and sprinkle with jelly, previously heated in a bain-marie.

INGREDIENTS

250 g flour
1 tablespoon vinegar
1 tablespoon oil
10 tablespoons water
1 teacup corn jelly
salt, flour and oil
to taste

SUGGESTION
Replace jelly by powdered sugar and cinnamon to sprinkle over the strips.

INGREDIENTS

2 tomatoes
1 teaspoon dry oregano
1 tablespoon grated
parmesan cheese
200 g light cream
cheese
2 aubergines
1 coffeespoon crushed
black pepper
50 ml olive oil
2 leaves lettuce
salt and black pepper
to taste

Aubergine rolls

Average
35 minutes
4

Turn on the oven at 180° C. Cut tomatoes into sections, season with salt and pepper and sprinkle with half the oregano. Bake tomatoes for 10 minutes in the oven and set aside. Mix the parmesan with the cream cheese and remaining oregano. Season with salt, and pepper and mix well. Refrigerate for 15 minutes.

Wash aubergines, slice into fine layers and season to taste. Let rest for a few minutes. Then, wash in water and dry well. Fry au-

bergine layers in hot olive oil, on both sides. Remove and drain on paper towel. Fill with cheese mixture and roll.

Cut the lettuce in Julienne and arrange in dishes. Place aubergine rolls on top, garnish with baked tomato and serve immediately.

Tofu meat balls

Easy

40 minutes

4

Grate the tofu and add it to the chopped onion and almond and pine nut kernels. Season with salt, pepper and soya sauce.

Cut the mixed flours bread into slices, lightly moisten with a few drops of water and mix in the remaining ingredients. Knead all and shape into small balls, brushing with beaten egg and then covering with breadcrumbs. Fry in hot oil, drain on absorbent paper and serve garnished with mint.

INGREDIENTS

300 g tofu
1 onion
2 tablespoons chopped
almond kernels
2 tablespoons pine nut
kernels
1 tablespoon soya sauce
250 g mixed flours bread
salt, pepper, beaten egg,
breadcrumbs, oil
and mint to taste

INGREDIENTS

600 g new potatoes
1 tablespoon oregano
1 teaspoon cumin
1 teaspoon pepper
1 leek
1 small red pepper
1 sprig spring onion
olive oil and black
olives to taste

Easy
50 minutes
4

Roast potatoes
with spring onion

Turn on the oven to 180° C. Cut the potatoes into medium sized cubes and season with oregano, cumin and pepper. Mix well and leave to rest for five minutes.

Husk and cut the leak into round slices along with the red pepper and potato pieces. Coat the bottom of a heat resistant container with olive oil and layer the leek, potatoes and red pepper.

Put in the oven for 30 minutes until the potatoes are soft. If necessary add a little more olive oil.

When time has elapsed, switch off the oven and sprinkle the preparation with chopped spring onion; keep in the heat for another five minutes. Remove and serve immediately, garnishing with stoned black olives.

Seitan steak

Cut the seitan very finely. Mix the water with the soya sauce, chopped garlic cloves and a laurel leaf. Add the seitan and leave to marinate for one hour.

Peel the potatoes and cut into slices. Fry them in plenty of oil, season with salt and leave to one side.

Fry the eggs in plenty of oil, turning them with a wooden spatula. Remove the seitan marinate and fry in the olive oil. Season with pepper and turn it when it gains colour. After it is cooked on both sides, refresh with the marinade and let boil. Remove and serve all together.

INGREDIENTS

300 g seitan
50 ml water
1 tablespoon of soya
sauce
2 cloves garlic
1 laurel leaf
800 g potatoes
4 eggs
50 ml olive oil
cooking oil
salt and pepper to taste

1 soya flour sausage
1 soya garlic sausage
1 soya chorizo
300 g potatoes
2 turnips
200 g savoy cabbage
200 g carrots
100 g rice
200 ml water
salt, pepper and parsley
to taste

Vegetarian bake

Easy

35 minutes

4

Prick the sausages with a fork and cook in plenty of water, seasoned with salt and pepper. After cooking, leave to one side, in the same water, and cook the vegetables, which have been cut into pieces.

Cook the rice in water seasoned with salt. Cut the sausages and arrange them diagonally over the vegetables and rice. Garnish with parsley and serve.

Fusilli with vegetables

Cook the pasta in plenty of water, seasoned with salt and pepper to taste; set aside. Cook the broccoli separately, also in water seasoned with salt and pepper; after cooling, slice into pieces.

Cut the pepper into small cubes and the carrots into rounds; stew in the olive oil. Season with salt and pepper. Add the broccoli and pasta and sprinkle with half the sesame seeds. Sprinkle with cream and soya sauce and mix. Sprinkle with the remaining sesame seed and serve.

INGREDIENTS

300 g fusilli
200 g broccoli
1/2 red pepper
100 g carrots
50 ml olive oil
3 tablespoons sesame seeds
200 ml soya cream
1 tablespoon soya sauce
salt and pepper to taste

INGREDIENTS

1 medium sized onion
2 cloves garlic
50 ml olive oil
1 laurel leaf
1 aubergine
1 courgette
1/2 green pepper
1/2 red pepper
300 g ripe tomatoes
100 ml white wine
300 g Greek tofu
salt and ground pepper
and lemon thyme
to taste

Tofu stew

Easy

35 minutes

4

Peel and chop the onion and the cloves of garlic. Peel, wash and cut the aubergine, courgette and red and green peppers into pieces. Stew the onion and garlic in olive oil in a frying pan with the laurel leaf, then add the aubergine, courgette and peppers. Season with salt and freshly ground pepper.

Add the peeled, seeded and chopped tomato. Add the white wine and leave to boil.

Add a little water to the stew and cook for 15 minutes. Cut the tofu into cubes and stir into the previous mixture. Cook for five minutes and sprinkle with chopped thyme.

Seitan jardinière

Stew the onion and garlic in olive oil. Cut the sausage into rounds and mix them into the stew. Then cook for a few minutes, adding the white wine and add tomato pulp. Season with salt and pepper.

Peel the potatoes and carrots and cut into cubes. Add them to the stew and cover with water. Arrange the green beans and cut into pieces. Also add the preparation and adjust the seasoning. Cover, then stew until soft and serve.

INGREDIENTS

2 tablespoons frozen
chopped onion
1 teaspoon frozen
chopped garlic
50 ml olive oil
1 seitan and tofu sausage
200 ml white wine
2 tablespoons tomato
pulp
600 g potatoes
200 g carrots
200 g green beans
salt and pepper to taste

INGREDIENTS

300 g lasagne sheets
2 carrots
300 g savoy cabbage
100 g green asparagus
100 g round green beans
1/2 courgette
2 cloves garlic
2 tablespoon olive oil
400 ml béchamel sauce
salt to taste

Green lasagne

Easy
30 minutes
4

Place a pan filled with salted water on the stove. When it begins to boil, add the sheets of pasta, one at a time. Leave them to cook for three minutes then set aside in cold water. Peel the carrots, slice into half moons and cook with the cabbage, julienne cut. Cut the remaining vegetables into pieces and cook them also.

Chop the garlic cloves and fry in the olive oil. Add the drained vegetables, season and sauté for a few minutes. Set the oven at 200º C. Then in a Pyrex dish, layer the vegetables, lasagne sheets and béchamel sauce, ending with the latter. Leave in the oven for 15 minutes. Remove from the heat and serve immediately.

Bulgur and italian tofu salad

Soak the bulgur in lukewarm water for 30 minutes. Cook the soya beans in salted water. Remove from the heat, drain and set aside. Peel the tomato, remove the seeds and chop it.

Also chop the cloves of garlic and onion, as well as the mint. Cut the Italian tofu into cubes and drain the bulgur. Mix all ingredients and season with salt and pepper and lemon juice. Mix and serve salad well chilled.

INGREDIENTS

300 g bulgur
150 g frozen soya beans
350 g ripe tomatoes
2 cloves garlic
1 medium onion
1 sprig mint
200 g Italian tofu
2 lemons (juice)
salt and pepper to taste

Corn salad

Easy
50 minutes
4

Soak the yellow canjica corn the day before and cook it in a pressure cooker for 25 minutes. Cook the soya beans and the peas separately, drain and leave to cool. Also cook the eggs in water for nine minutes. After cooking, shell them, chop coarsely and leave to one side.

Peel the carrots, cut into small cubes and also cook in water seasoned with salt. Cut the red pepper into small pieces and drain the maize, then cook it and leave to cool afterwards.

Mix all prepared ingredients in a salad bowl and season with salt, pepper, olive oil and a little cider vinegar. Serve the salad sprinkled with the cooked and chopped eggs.

Tofu stir fry

Easy

30 minutes

6

Cut the tofu into fine strips and set aside. Also cut the onions and the cloves of garlic into strips and fry them in olive oil. Season with salt, pepper and the laurel leaf.

When the onions are tender, add the tofu and leave to stew. Mix in the potatoes; beat the eggs and add them also. Mix all very well, season with salt, pepper and let cook to taste. Remove, sprinkle with chopped parsley and serve.

INGREDIENTS

200 g tofu
2 medium onions
2 cloves garlic
50 ml olive oil
1 laurel leaf
400 g fried potato
sticks
4 eggs
1 sprig chopped parsley
salt and pepper to taste

Easy

20 minutes

4

Smoked tofu
with rose pepper sauce

Cut the smoked tofu into small slices; grill slowly along with the cherry tomato. Wash the lettuce leaves and julienne cut them. Grate the radishes and drain the corn. Arrange these ingredients on a plate and sprinkle with chopped thyme, half of the rose pepper and olive oil.

Arrange the grilled tofu on a serving dish, sprinkle with thyme and season with the remaining pepper and olive oil. Sprinkle with balsamic cream to taste and serve accompanied by the salad and grilled tomatoes, also sprinkled with thyme.

Grilled tofu
with courgette

Wash the courgettes, dry them and cut into rounds; season with salt, pepper and a little olive oil. Place on a grill to heat and cook the vegetables.

Season the slices of tofu in the same way and grill them also. Apportion on individual plates and sprinkle with sesame seeds. Garnish with sprigs of basil and serve immediately with sweet red berries.

INGREDIENTS

2 courgettes
100 ml olive oil
4 slices tofu
1 tablespoon sesame seeds
1 sprig basil
1 tablespoon sweet red berries
salt and pepper to taste

TO ACCOMPANY

Stew two tablespoonfuls of frozen onion and a little frozen chopped garlic with a trickle of sunflower oil in a pressure cooker. Add 300 g of wholegrain rice, 50 g of peas and 600 ml of water; season with salt, close the pressure cooker and cook for 20 minutes.

Easy

30 minutes

4

Breaded tofu
with sesame

Cut the tofu into slices; marinate in Soya sauce and lemon juice, sprinkled with garlic powder. Leave to marinate for 30 minutes, drain and coat with flour, beaten egg and sesame seeds. Fry in hot oil and drain on paper towel.

Peel and grate the carrot. Cut the fennel into fine strips and rip the lettuce. Mix both ingredients with the carrots and raisins. Sprinkle with a little sunflower oil and season with salt. Serve the breaded tofu with salad.

Chinese noodles
with soya bean sprouts

Wash the courgette and leek. Cut into slices. Peel the carrot and cut in the same way. Also wash the orange pepper and remove its seeds; cut into layers and set aside. Rinse the Soya bean sprouts under running water and drain. Cook the chinese noodles in boiling water, seasoned with salt, for two minutes.

Put a pan containing a little olive oil on the stove; add the vegetables and crushed garlic. Cover and leave to stew over a gentle heat, stirring occasionally.

Drain the noodles when cooked and add the vegetables. Season with salt, pepper and sprinkle with Soya sauce to taste and mix in. Serve immediately.

INGREDIENTS

1 courgette
100 g leek
1 large carrot
1 orange pepper
1 tin Soya bean sprouts
250 g chinese noodles
1 clove garlic
salt, olive oil, pepper
and Soya sauce to taste

INGREDIENTS

200 ml Soya cream
2 eggs
2 large potatoes
1 large carrot
1 medium courgette
1 onion
1 sprig fresh oregano
salt, pepper,
nutmeg, powdered garlic
and butter to taste

Vegetables au gratin

Medium
45 minutes
4

Set the oven at 180º C. Mix the cream with the eggs in a bowl; season with salt, pepper, nutmeg and powdered garlic. Add a few small leaves of fresh oregano and set aside. Cut the potatoes, carrot and courgette into fine slices with a mandoline slicer and blend them in with the cream mixture.

Peel and cut the onion into half moons; also add to the previous preparation. Mix all very well and transfer to a Pyrex dish, greased with butter. Place in a pre-heated oven for 30 minutes. Remove and serve very hot.

Soya bolognese

Cook the pasta in water, seasoned with salt and a trickle of oil. Heat the Bolognese with a little water and add chopped ginger. Remove from the heat and leave to cool.

Add a pinch of sweet basil to the Bolognese and stir well. Serve over the cooked asparagus and sprinkle with grated cheese to taste. Garnish with basil.

INGREDIENTS

300 g spinach
and tomato spaghetti
4 packets Soya
Bolognese
1 teaspoon fresh ginger
salt, oil, parmesan
cheese and basil
to taste

SUGGESTION
When adding the ginger,
also add a small tin of
rolled mushrooms.

INGREDIENTS

6 dried mushrooms
100 g snow peas
100 g Brussels sprouts
2 carrots
50 ml olive oil
1 tin baby corn ears
1 tin Soya bean sprouts
1 malagueta pepper
2 tablespoons freshly
chopped herbs
100 ml sunflower oil
50 ml cider vinegar
1 teaspoon mustard
salt and pepper to taste

Mixed vegetables
with vinaigrette

Medium
25 minutes
4

Soak the mushrooms in warm water for 20 minutes to hydrate. Arrange the vegetables and cook them separately in salted water; drain and set aside.

Drain the mushrooms and cut into pieces. Place a frying pan with olive oil on medium heat. Add the mushrooms and sauté

them. Then add the baby corn, Soya bean sprouts, malagueta and cooked vegetables; let sit.

Grind the fresh herbs together with the oil, cider vinegar and mustard. Season with salt and pepper. Pour this vinaigrette over the sautéed vegetables and serve.

Mixed salad

Rip the lettuce and cut the tomatoes into cubes. Place both in a salad bowl and set aside. Cut the tofu and cheese into cubes. Chop the onion and green pepper. Grate the carrot and mix all in the salad bowl.

Add the olives and walnut. Season the salad with salt, pepper, olive oil, vinegar and oregano. Mix. Lastly, mix in the yoghurt and serve.

INGREDIENTS

1 lettuce
2 medium tomatoes
250 g tofu
100 g parmesan cheese
1/2 onion
1 green pepper
1 grated carrot
50 g stoned black olives
2 tablespoons walnut kernels
1 skimmed natural yoghurt
salt, pepper, olive oil, vinegar and oregano to taste

6 medium potatoes
2 green peppers
3 carrots
4 artichoke hearts
100 g leek
1 turnip
8 tablespoons olive oil
1 onion
3 cloves of garlic
1 tablespoon flour
1 packet tofu
2 laurel leaves
1 cup white wine
1 tablespoon Soya sauce
1 tablespoon chopped parsley
salt and coarse black pepper to taste

Soya and tofu stew

Easy
35 minutes
4

Cut the potatoes, peppers, carrots, artichokes, leek and turnip into pieces. Place the olive oil in a pan on the stove and sauté the artichokes lightly; remove the fat and set aside. Fry the onion and cloves of garlic in the same olive oil and then the remaining vegetables, except for the potatoes. Leave to cook until they gain colour; sprinkle with the flour and mix.

Cut the tofu into cubes and add the vegetables, as well as the laurel and white wine. Season with salt and pepper; cover the pan and leave to simmer gently. Add the potatoes and sufficient water to cook. After they are cooked, add the artichokes; season with Soya sauce and leave to cook for five minutes. Remove, sprinkle with chopped parsley and serve.

MAIN DISHES

Seitan mille-feuilles

Peel the onion and cloves of garlic then chop. Heat the olive oil on low heat and fry the sliced seitan together with the onion and garlic; season with salt, pepper and Soya sauce. Drain the seitan of the fat; leave aside and add chopped tomato. Sprinkle with oregano, leave to stew a little and add the wine as it starts to dry. Mash the sauce and set aside.

Heat the oven to 170° C. Prepare the croquettes, spreading a portion of almonds on to a silicon tray. Sprinkle with salt and sugar. Place in the oven until they begin to colour and the sugar melts; leave to cool. Make the mille feuilles, layering the croquettes with arugula and seitan. Serve with tomato sauce.

INGREDIENTS

1 small onion
2 cloves garlic
50 ml olive oil
400 g seitan
1 teaspoon Soya sauce
80 g peeled tomatoes
1 teaspoon oregano
100 ml white wine
80 g rolled almond
kernels
salt, sugar and arugula
to taste

6 fresh lasagne sheets
1 onion
2 tablespoons vegetable butter
200 g red cabbage
200 g carrots
100 ml white wine
100 g Soya bean sprouts
200 ml vegetable cream
2 tablespoons ketchup
salt to taste

Vegetable cannelloni

Medium

1 hour

4

Place the lasagne sheets in a pan on the stove and cook with plenty of water, seasoned with salt, for two minutes. Remove; place in cold water and set aside. Meanwhile set the oven at 180º C.

Cut the onion into half moons and fry them in butter. Julienne cut the red cabbage and carrot and add them to the stew. Leave to simmer gently. Add the wine; leave to reduce and add the soya bean sprouts; mix in and set aside.

Cut each pasta sheet in half, distribute the vegetables on them, roll up and place in a heat resistant container. Mix the cream in with the ketchup and pour over the cannelloni. Place in the oven for 10 minutes. Remove and serve hot.

Vegetarian stew

Peel and chop the onion and garlic cloves; fry them in palm oil. Cut the tofu into cubes and add to the mix. Season with salt and pepper.

Peel and cut the carrots into rounds, and cut the artichokes into slices. Add them to the tofu preparation, blending delicately so as not to divide the tofu. Leave to cook.

Add the white wine and the peeled, chopped and seedless tomatoes. Boil for five minutes more, stirring from time to time. Mix in the beans and leave to boil again. Remove and serve the stew, sprinkled with chopped parsley.

INGREDIENTS

1 small onion
2 cloves garlic
1 tablespoon palm oil
200 g tofu
100 g carrots
180 g canned artichoke
hearts
100 ml white wine
100 g peeled tomatoes
500 g cooked red beans
1 sprig parsley
salt and pepper to taste

SUGGESTION
Replace the artichokes
with 200 grams
of mushrooms
sliced in half.

INGREDIENTS

1.5 kg potatoes
1 coffeespoon nutmeg
1 onion
1 clove garlic
200 g mushrooms
2 carrots
2 courgettes
1 stalk raw celery
1/2 leeks
1 tin corn
50 ml white wine
2 eggs
salt, pepper and olive oil
to taste

Vegetable patty

Easy
40 minutes
4

Set the oven at 200° C. Cook the potatoes in plenty of water then drain. Reduce to a purée and season with salt, pepper and nutmeg; set aside.

Chop the onion and clove of garlic; fry in a little olive oil. Cut the carrots, courgettes, celery and leek into cubes. Add the vegetables to the mixture together with the maize and white wine. Stir and leave to cook.

Cover the base of a baking tray with the purée, layer the vegetable preparation and finish with more purée. Brush the surface with beaten egg and leave to cook au gratin in the top part of the oven.

Egg and potato vegetables

Cut the onions into half moons and chop the garlic clove. Julienne cut the carrots, courgettes and celery. Stew all in olive oil. Season with salt and pepper.

Add the chip sticks and mix. Beat the eggs and add them to the mixture so they do not stick. Sprinkle with chopped parsley and olives.

INGREDIENTS

2 onions
1 clove garlic
100 ml olive oil
2 carrots
2 courgettes
1 horseradish-celery
1 packet bread sticks
4 eggs
1 tablespoon round black olives
salt, pepper, oil
and chopped parsley
to taste

INGREDIENTS

4 leaves Savoy cabbage
150 g rice
1 tablespoon butter
1 clove garlic
1 onion
50 ml olive oil
2 ripe tomatoes
100 ml white wine
1 tablespoon
tomato pulp
200 g seitan
salt, Soya sauce
and oregano to taste

Medium
50 minutes
4

Savoy Cabbage
wedges with seitan

Set the oven at 200° C. Cook the cabbage leaves and allow to drain. Cook the rice, for 12 minutes, with twice as much water seasoned with salt. When ready, add the butter and mix in.

Chop the garlic and onion and fry in the olive oil. Remove the skins and seeds from the tomatoes. Add them to the stew and mix in. Add the wine and the pulp of the tomatoes and as soon as it boils, remove from the heat. Divide the mixture into two parts.

Add the chopped seitan to one of these parts, season with Soya sauce and leave to cook for five minutes.

Place the preparation in the centre of the Savoy cabbage leaves and roll up. Arrange the wedges on a tray and cook in the oven for 10 minutes. Mash the remaining part of the mixture and add a little oregano; mix in and adjust the seasoning. Serve the wedges with rice and tomato sauce.

Vegetable and soya bean sprout salad

Mix the butter beans with the Soya bean sprouts and sweet-corn in a container. Chop the radishes and add them to the previous mixture.

Season with salt, pepper, olive oil, vinegar and parsley. Adjust the seasoning and serve.

INGREDIENTS

200 g tinned butter beans
100 g canned Soya bean sprouts
100 g tinned sweet-corn
2 radishes
50 ml olive oil
3 tablespoons vinegar
1 sprig parsley
salt and pepper to taste

Ciabatta with tofu and vegetables

Easy
30 minutes
4

Mix the flour with the sugar, yeast, salt and grated Parmesan. Then add the water and butter. Knead until a mouldable and homogenous preparation is obtained. Leave to leaven for a few minutes.

Remove the seeds from the peppers and cut them into cubes as well as the tofu. Season with salt, pepper, oregano and olive oil. Set the oven at 180° C, and grease a baking tray with butter.

Roll out the dough and place it on the baking tray. Put in the oven for 35 minutes. Trim the top of the ciabatta and cover it with the tomato sauce. Arrange the prepared ingredients on top, sprinkle with grated cheese and serve.

Tofu salad
with balsamic vinegar

Cut the tofu into small cubes and place them in a bowl. Chop the onion and cut the tomatoes into cubes, after removing the seeds. Add the corn, Soya bean sprouts, chopped onion and tomato cubes to the tofu.

Remove the peel and seeds from the cucumber; cut into cubes and add them to the remaining ingredients. Season the salad with salt, olive oil and balsamic vinegar to taste. Mix and serve.

INGREDIENTS

400 g tofu
100 g Soya bean sprouts
1 red onion
2 tomatoes
100 g cooked corn
1 cucumber
2 tablespoons olive oil
salt and balsamic vinegar
to taste

COOKING SUGGESTION
Serve with a little tonkatsu sauce, made from Worcestershire sauce, Soya sauce, sake, etc.

INGREDIENTS

250 g bulgur
4 gherkins
1 tablespoon stoned
black olives
4 tomatoes
1 sprig mint
2 fresh cheeses
2 lemons (juice)
salt, pepper and olive oil
to taste

Bulgur salad

Easy
40 minutes
4

Soak the bulgur in cold water for 30 minutes. Slice the gherkins and the black olives.

Wash and remove the seeds in half of the tomatoes; cut into small cubes. Wash and chop the mint. Cut the fresh cheese into small cubes.

Mix all of the ingredients and season with salt, pepper, olive oil and lemon juice. Serve the salad chilled, garnished with the remaining tomatoes, cut into sections.

MAIN DISHES

Vegetable tofu

Cut the tofu into cubes; marinate with olive oil, Soya sauce, saffron and a teaspoon of curry. Season with salt, pepper and fresh herbs; leave to gather flavour for 15 minutes. Put the rice on the stove to cook in plenty of water, seasoned with salt, for 12 minutes, adding the drained black beans.

Wash and cut the red pepper into small cubes, carrots into rounds, green beans into slices and Chinese cabbage into pieces. Peel the mango and cut into slices. Heat the olive oil in a wok and add the chopped onion, sliced garlic, tofu drained from the marinade and the remaining curry powder. Stir until the onion becomes transparent.

Add the broccoli, carrots, green beans and Chinese cabbage to the mixture; leave to fry until it has a strong colour, covering the wok. Remove from the stove and add the red pepper, mango, chopped coriander and pepper to taste; mix. Distribute the rice with the black beans onto plates and accompany with the mixed vegetables and fried tofu. Sprinkle with toasted almonds and serve.

INGREDIENTS

150 g tofu
2 tablespoons olive oil
3 tablespoons Soya sauce
1 teaspoon saffron
4 teaspoons curry powder
1 teacup rice
1 tin black beans
1 red pepper
2 medium carrots
10 shelled green beans
50 g Chinese cabbage
4 cloves garlic
1/2 onion
1 mango
50 ml olive oil
4 sprigs broccoli
1 sprig coriander
3 tablespoons toasted almonds,
salt, coarse pepper and fresh herbs to taste

INGREDIENTS

200 g tofu
2 dl of water
1 tablespoon of stirred
soja paste
1 sprig of spring onion
2 cloves of garlic
1 small carrot
1/2 red pepper
1 tablespoon
of sesame oil
salt, pepper and lettuce
leaves to taste

Lettuce and tofu roll

Easy

30 minutes

4

Cut the tofu into small cubes; stew in water together with the Soya paste, spring onion and garlic cloves, both chopped. Thinly slice the carrot and red pepper into small pieces; add to the preparation.

Leave to simmer gently for 10 minutes. Add the sesame oil half way through. Following this, leave to cool and roll the preparation into the lettuce leaves. Keep cold until serving.

Seitan chowder

Easy
30 minutes
4

Cut the seitan into slices. Peel the potatoes and onions. Slice the potatoes, onions, tomatoes and peppers into rounds, removing the seeds. Arrange the ingredients in layers in a pan; season with salt, pepper and coriander. Add the white wine and leave to cook for 10 minutes, covering the pan. Adjust the seasoning and serve.

INGREDIENTS

250 g seitan
600 g potatoes
2 small onions
3 tomatoes
1 green pepper
1 red pepper
1 sprig coriander
200 ml white wine
salt and pepper to taste

SUGGESTION
Add 100 grams
of chopped Soya
chorizo
to the chowder.

Fresh cheese chowder

Easy
30 minutes
4

Cut the previously seeded tomatoes and peppers, cloves of garlic, onions and fresh cheese into rounds. Then, cut the cabbage into pieces.

Place all ingredients in a pan in layers, except the garlic. Season with salt, pepper and garlic. Add the white wine and put on the stove. Cover and leave to cook for 10 minutes.

Slice the bread; spread with butter and sprinkle on the oregano. Put it on the top shelf of the oven at 180° C, and toast it. Serve the bread with the chowder.

Soya cannelloni

Easy

50 minutes

4

Soak the Soya in plenty of tepid water for 10 minutes. Place a container containing water, salt and a trickle of olive oil on the stove. When it boils, add the cannelloni and cook for five minutes. Remove and set aside.

Turn on the oven to 200° C. Chop the onion and cloves of garlic. Fry them in the olive oil. Following this, add the drained Soya and the peeled, chopped and seeded tomatoes. After five minutes, add the wine and leave to cook for a further 10 minutes.

Drain the previously prepared mixture and add half of the béchamel to it. Mix well and stuff the cannelloni. Place it on a heat resistant tray and cover it with the remaining béchamel and olives. Place on the upper shelf of the oven to cook au gratin. Serve, garnished to taste.

INGREDIENTS

90 g fine Soya
16 dry cannelloni
1 onion
3 cloves garlic
50 ml olive oil
1 small tin tomatoes
100 ml white wine
500 ml béchamel sauce
2 tablespoons olives
in rounds
salt and oil to taste

SUGGESTION

Place the prepared
Soya at the bottom
of the baking tray,
cover with potato
and carrot purée
and place in
the oven.

Easy

35 minutes

4

Vegetable lasagne

Wash the vegetables. Peel the carrots and cut them into small cubes, together with the peppers and courgettes. Separate the broccoli into stems. Cook all in salted water. Cook the lasagne pasta in water, seasoned with salt and a tablespoon of olive oil for three minutes.

Sauté the vegetables in the remaining olive oil and add in the cream. Season with salt and pepper. Leave to thicken a little. Place alternate layers of lasagne and vegetables on a heat resistant tray, ending with the pasta. Sprinkle with mozzarella cheese and place on the upper shelf in the oven to cook au gratin.

MAIN DISHES

Spaghetti
with aubergine and garlic

Cook the spaghetti in plenty of water, seasoned with salt and a trickle of olive oil; drain and keep hot.

Wash the aubergines. Dry them on paper towels and then cut into small cubes. Brown them in the olive oil together with the peeled and chopped cloves of garlic. Add the chopped marjoram; season with salt and pepper.

Accompany the spaghetti with the aubergine preparation and serve hot, garnished with croutons.

INGREDIENTS

280 g spaghetti
2 aubergines
50 ml olive oil
5 cloves garlic
1 sprig marjoram
olive oil, salt, pepper
and croutons to taste

SUGGESTION
Add 250 grams of
cream or fresh
cheese to the pasta.

150 ml olive oil
1 sprig coriander
1 clove garlic
500 g dry cheese ravioli
4 cherry tomatoes
salt and oil to taste

Ravioli with coriander olive oil

Easy
30 minutes
4

Heat the olive oil in a frying pan and add the chopped coriander and crushed garlic. Remove from the heat; after five minutes, filter the olive oil with a fine net sieve and set aside.

Cook the ravioli in plenty of water, seasoned with salt and a trickle of oil. Drain it and arrange on a plate. Add the reserved olive oil and garnish with the cherry tomatoes.

Farfalle with vegetables

Cook the pasta in plenty of water, seasoned with salt. Half way through cooking, add the split peas. Peel the tomato, removing the seeds and cutting it into small pieces.

Heat the oil and fry the chopped onion and cloves of garlic. Add the tomato, pasta, peas and sliced mushrooms. Sauté on very high heat and season with salt and pepper. Serve.

INGREDIENTS

450 g three colour
farfalle
250 g mushy peas
3 tomatoes
100 ml olive oil
1 onion
4 cloves garlic
200 g tinned mushrooms
salt and pepper to taste

SUGGESTION
Serve the pasta
with mayonnaise, cooked
green asparagus,
sweet corn and broad
beans.

INGREDIENTS

400 g spinach and
cheese tortellini
150 g baby corn ears
200 g cherry tomatoes
400 g mushrooms
4 tablespoons olive oil
1 teaspoon dry wild
oregano
2 dl of Soya cream
1 tablespoon Antigua
mustard
salt, olive oil and pepper
to taste

SUGGESTION
Grill four slices
of tofu to accompany.

Easy

30 minutes

4

Tortellini
with mustard sauce

Cook the pasta in plenty of water, seasoned with salt and olive oil. Wash the baby corn, cherry tomatoes and mushrooms; drain and add the olive oil. Season with salt, pepper and oregano; grill.

Mix the cream with the mustard and place on the stove to thicken. Accompany the pasta with the vegetables and pour the sauce over all when serving.

Maccaroni pie

Cook the pasta in water, seasoned with salt and a trickle of oil. Defrost and chop the spinach. Soak the apricots and sultanas in tepid water. Mix the spinach, apricots, sultanas and béchamel sauce in a container; season with salt and pepper.

Set the oven at 200° C. Place a layer of pasta on a heat resistant tray, pour on the spinach preparation and end with the remaining pasta. Sprinkle with the cheese and place on the upper shelf of the oven to cook au gratin.

INGREDIENTS

600 g striped macaroni
350 g cooked frozen
   spinach
120 g dried apricots
120 g black sultanas
400 ml béchamel sauce
150 g emmental cheese
salt, oil and pepper
   to taste

SUGGESTION
Add a teaspoon
of saffron
to the pasta water.

INGREDIENTS

450 g fusilli pasta
250 g baby carrots
250 g peas
400 ml béchamel sauce
200 g mozzarella cheese
salt, oil and pepper
to taste

Spring fusilli

Easy
35 minutes
4

Cook the pasta in plenty of water, seasoned with salt and a trickle of oil. Cook the vegetables separately in salted water for eight minutes. Mix the pasta with the vegetables and add the béchamel sauce.

Pour the mixture into a heat resistant tray; season with salt, pepper and sprinkle with the grated cheese. Place on the top shelf of the oven, set at 200° C, to cook au gratin. Remove and serve.

Seitan coriander

Make a marinade with the olive oil, chopped coriander, chopped garlic cloves, salt and pepper. Cut the seitan into cubes and add to the marinade, leaving to rest for 40 minutes.

Slice the potatoes into rounds and cook them in water with salt. Drain the olive oil from the marinade and place it on the stove with the chopped onion. Stew. Cut the carrots into half moons; add to the stew and adjust the seasoning.

Add the seitan and the coriander marinade; leave to colour a little and sprinkle with flour. Mix all very well and add the water and wine, leaving to thicken. Finally, add the potatoes and serve.

INGREDIENTS

50 ml olive oil
1 sprig coriander
4 cloves garlic
250 g seitan
600 g potatoes
1 small onion
300 g carrots
100 ml water
100 ml white wine
salt, pepper
and flour to taste

Easy //
30 minutes
4

Chinese noodles
with tofu

Cook the noodles in water, seasoned with salt for approximately seven minutes; drain and set aside. Cut the tofu into small cubes and fry in the oil. Stir to gain colour on both sides. Adjust the seasoning.

Cut the onion into cubes; add to the preparation and leave to stew a little. Chop the peeled and seeded tomato; add this also. Leave to thicken and add the cooked pasta. Blend and serve with the sprig of coriander.

Vegetable kebabs

Cut the aubergine, courgette, mushrooms and red pepper into pieces. Take the stalks out of the cherry tomatoes and wash them. Alternate the vegetables onto the skewers.

Season the kebabs with salt and grill. Prepare the sauce, grinding the cloves of garlic. Add the olive oil and coriander to it; season with salt and pepper. Serve the grilled vegetables covered with the sauce.

INGREDIENTS

1 small aubergine
1 courgette
150 g mushrooms
1 red pepper
150 g cherry tomatoes
2 cloves garlic
100 ml olive oil
1 tablespoon fresh
coriander
salt and pepper to taste

SUGGESTION
Before serving, sprinkle the kebabs with poppy seeds.

200 g lasagne pasta
70 g vegetable butter
80 g flour
1 l Soya milk
1 coffeespoon nutmeg
200 g finely granulated
Soya
50 ml olive oil
1 small onion
2 cloves garlic
1 ripe tomato
2 tablespoons
tomato pulp
1 laurel leaf
1 sprig thyme
1 sprig oregano
1 sprig parsley
100 ml white wine
300 ml water
1 large red onion
50 g Parmesan cheese
salt and pepper to taste

Red onion lasagne

Easy
40 minutes
6

Cook the lasagne sheets in salted water; drain and set aside. Soften the butter and add flour to it. Add the Soya milk mixing continuously; season with salt and nutmeg; cook for 10 minutes, stirring continuously, until it thickens.

Cook the Soya in the olive oil; add the onion rings and chopped garlic cloves. Lower the heat and leave to cook; season with salt and pepper. Add the chopped tomato and pulp; season with the laurel leaf, thyme, oregano and chopped parsley. Add the wine and leave to boil. Add the water; cover the pan and cook for a further 20 minutes.

Place a layer of the pasta on a tray and then a layer of the Soya preparation and then the béchamel. Repeat this and end with the béchamel sauce; sprinkle with grated Parmesan cheese and red onion rings. Place in the oven at 200° C, for ten minutes to cook au gratin. Then serve.

Tofu aromatised with olive oil

Cut the tofu into cubes; season with olive oil and chopped coriander. Wash and cut the tomatoes into cubes; set aside. Drain the olive oil from the tofu and heat it.

Add the tofu again; when it has been cooked, add the sliced garlic. Cook a little more; season with salt and pepper and serve with assorted lettuce.

INGREDIENTS

200 g tofu
50 ml olive oil
1 sprig coriander
1 tomato
2 cloves garlic
salt, pepper and assorted
lettuce to taste

SUGGESTION
Add a tablespoon
of chopped olives
to the mixture.

Stuffed potatoes

Easy
40 minutes
4

Wash the potatoes well and wrap them in aluminium foil. Place them in the oven at 180° C, for 20 minutes. Soak the granulated Soya in cold water for 20 minutes.

Chop the cloves of garlic and the onion; stew in the olive oil. Add the well drained and chopped granulated Soya. Season with salt and pepper; add the béchamel sauce and egg yolks to bind well. Add the parsley and red pepper, both chopped.

Cut the potatoes in half in a full-length direction; remove the pulp without damaging the skin.

Stuff each half with the Soya preparation and arrange the other half on top. Rewrap them in the aluminium foil and place in the oven again, for 15 minutes. Serve with the tomatoes and lemon herbs.

Mixed vegetables
with cheese

Easy

25 minutes

4

Arrange the vegetables and cut them into pieces. Cook them separately in salted water; drain and place on a baking tray.

Sprinkle with olive oil and add the cloves of garlic, slightly crushed with the peel, and place the cheese, cut into small pieces, on top.

Season with salt and pepper and place in the oven, set at 180° C, for 10 minutes. Serve sprinkled with chopped coriander.

INGREDIENTS

200 g cauliflower
200 g carrots
300 g broccoli
100 ml olive oil
3 cloves garlic
100 g cheese
1 tablespoon
freshly chopped
coriander
salt and pepper to taste

Baked aubergines

Easy
30 minutes
4

Set the oven at 180° C. Wash and coarsely chop the tomatoes, onion and cloves of garlic; cook in a little olive oil. Add the water; season with salt, pepper and leave to cook for approximately 10 minutes. Mash the mixture and pass it through a sieve.

Wash the aubergines well and cut into fine slices. Place a little of the prepared tomato sauce at the bottom of a heat resistant container; add a layer of aubergines, then the finely sliced seitan and then another layer of the aubergines and tomato sauce on top. Repeat this until the ingredients are all used, ending with the tomato sauce. Place in an oven for 20 minutes. Remove and serve hot.

MAIN DISHES

Soya and azuki stew

Soak the beans the day before in salted water. Cook them in a pressure cooker for 20 minutes, using the same water and half an onion, garlic and laurel. Set aside.

Stew the remaining onion, as well as the cloves of garlic, both chopped, separately, in the olive oil. Leave to colour a little and add the peppers, chopped tomatoes, carrots cut into rounds and the granulated Soya. Leave all to colour, mixing the ingredients well. Season with salt, pepper and the rest of the laurel leaf.

Add the white wine and broth from the beans. Cover the pan and leave to simmer for 20 minutes. Stir from time to time. Add the remaining beans and leave to boil. Serve, sprinkled with chopped coriander.

INGREDIENTS

150 g azuki beans
2 small onions
4 cloves garlic
2 laurel leaves
50 ml olive oil
1 green pepper
1 red pepper
2 small tomatoes
2 medium carrots
2 cups granulated Soya
100 ml white wine
1 sprig chopped coriander
salt and pepper to taste

SUGGESTION
Add a coffeespoon of coarse cumin to the stew, when it is cooking.

Seitan chop-suey

Easy /////
30 minutes
4

Cut the seitan into small fine slices and fry in olive oil. Season with salt and pepper; add the vegetables. Stir well and mix the ingredients over high heat.

Mix the water, flour and Soya sauce separately. Pour over the seitan preparation. Leave to stew for six minutes stirring continuously.

Ventagli
with rainbow vegetables

Cook the ventagli and broccoli separately in plenty of water; set aside. Beat the eggs and place them in a frying pan with butter, moulding into a crepe; roll it up and cut into slices; set aside.

Chop the onion, cloves of garlic and stew them in a little sesame oil. Add the carrots in small cubes and leave to stew for a little longer.

Cut the egg preparation into smaller pieces and mix into the stew; season with salt and pepper. Chop the broccoli and mix this into the preparation also. Serve the vegetables with the noodles, garnished with frittered beetroot.

INGREDIENTS

300 g ventagli
100 g broccoli
3 eggs
1 onion
2 cloves garlic
100 ml sesame oil
2 carrots
frittered beetroot,
butter, salt
and pepper to taste

SUGGESTION
Add 100 grams of
Cubed Parmesan cheese
to the recipe.

INGREDIENTS

200 g cooked butter
beans
400 g bread
1 sprig chopped parsley
1 chopped small onion
2 chopped cloves garlic
50 ml olive oil
1 laurel leaf
salt, pepper, flour,
sunflower oil, lettuce,
cherry tomatoes
and endive leaves to taste

SUGGESTION

Add two tablespoons
chopped peanuts to the
stew.

Easy

30 minutes

4

Bean escallops

Grind the beans with the bread and parsley; season with salt and set aside. Stew the onion and garlic cloves in the olive oil; season with salt, pepper and laurel. Leave to thicken a little and mix in the bean preparation.

After drying out a little, place on a tray and smooth with a spatula. Place in the refrigerator to solidify and then cut into rectangles. Cover with flour and fry in the oil. Serve the escallops with lettuce, cherry tomatoes and endive leaves.

Vegetarian patty

Cook the rice in salted water; drain and leave to cool. Cut the vegetables into small pieces and scald them. Stew the onion and the cloves of garlic, both chopped, in the olive oil. Leave to gain flavour and season with salt and pepper.

Place a layer of rice, one of vegetables and another of rice on a heat resistant tray. Sprinkle with cheese and cover with the cream whisked with eggs. Place the tray in the oven set at 180° C for 30 minutes. Remove and serve.

INGREDIENTS

350 g rice
200 g carrots
100 g broccoli
1/2 red pepper
1/2 green pepper
1 leek
50 ml olive oil
1 onion
3 cloves garlic
100 g grated flamengo cheese
200 ml Soya cream
2 eggs
salt and pepper to taste

SUGGESTION
Before covering with cream, sprinkle the patty with breadcrumbs.

INGREDIENTS

3 medium carrots
1 red pepper
300 g green beans
300 g spaghetti
1/2 medium onion
2 cloves garlic
50 ml olive oil
salt and pepper to taste

SUGGESTION
Add a chopped, peeled
and seedless ripe tomato
and a teaspoon
of red pepper paste
to the stew.

Easy
30 minutes
4

Spaghetti with vegetables

Peel the carrots and cut them into small cubes, as well as the pepper. Arrange the green beans and cut them into fine slices. Scald the carrots and the green beans in plenty of salted water; drain well and set aside.

Cook the spaghetti separately in salted water, until it is al dente. Cool under running water and drain well.

Chop the onion and the cloves of garlic and stew them in the olive oil. Add all of the vegetables; season with salt and finally stir in the spaghetti.

Squash lasagne
with dried fruit

Peel the squash, cut into pieces and cook in plenty of water; drain well and reduce to a purée.

Cook the lasagne sheets until they are al dente, drain and set aside. Chop the onion and cloves of garlic and stew in olive oil together with the almonds and raisins. Season with salt and leave to sit a little; leave aside. Mix the squash purée with the cream cheese; season with salt, pepper and nutmeg; set aside.

Grease a heat resistant container with butter and line the base with the lasagne sheets. Alternately layer the squash purée, dried fruit preparation, béchamel sauce and grated mozzarella cheese. Repeat until the ingredients are all used, ending with the grated cheese. Place in an oven set at 160° C for 30 minutes.

INGREDIENTS

800 g squash
300 g lasagne sheets
1 medium onion
3 cloves garlic
50 ml olive oil
60 g raisins
60 g chopped
almond kernels
200 g cream cheese
400 ml béchamel sauce
100 g grated
mozzarella cheese
salt, pepper,
nutmeg and butter
to taste

INGREDIENTS

50 ml olive oil
1 onion
2 cloves garlic
300 g arboreal rice
800 ml hot water
150 g chopped walnuts
1 sprig parsley
salt and pepper to taste

SUGGESTION

Replace the walnuts
with mushrooms
and add a small packet
of vegetable cream,
seasoned with a pinch
of paprika.

Easy
25 minutes
4

Walnut risotto

Heat the olive oil and stew the onion and chopped cloves of garlic. Add the rice to fry and season; after three minutes, add a little water. Cook on a very low heat for 18 minutes. Finally add the walnuts and the chopped parsley.

Vegetable paella

Easy

45 minutes

4

Chop the onion and the cloves of garlic and stew them in the olive oil in the paella pan. Add the rice and then the saffron. Blend well and add the carrots and peas.

Pour in a little water, according to the requirements of the rice. After four minutes, add the mushrooms and the beans; mix in and season. Cook for 10 minutes and turn off the heat; place the sliced morrone pepper on top and garnish with olives.

INGREDIENTS

1 onion
3 cloves garlic
50 ml olive oil
250 g steamed rice
1 teaspoon saffron
120 g baby carrots
120 g peas
600 ml hot water
1 small tin sliced
mushrooms
1 small tin red beans
1 morrone pepper
salt, pepper
and olives to taste

SUGGESTION
Substitute the beans with the same quantity of small cubed seitan.

INGREDIENTS

50 ml olive oil
280 g Thai rice
1 onion
2 cloves garlic
600 ml hot water
1/2 orange pepper
in small cubes
150 g runner beans
150 g sweet corn
salt and pepper to taste

SUGGESTION
Add 180 grams
of cheese
pieces to the rice
at the end.

Aromatic pilaf

Easy //
25 minutes
4

Heat the oil and fry the rice for five minutes on low heat, stirring continuously. Add the onion and the chopped cloves of garlic. Pour in the water, pepper, beans and the corn. Season to taste and simmer gently for 12 minutes. Serve hot.

Jambalaya

Chop the onion and garlic and stew them in a little olive oil. Add water and the peeled tomatoes, okras, baby corn, cut in half, and the kidney beans; season to taste.

Let cook for 10 minutes and add the rice. Cover and let cook for a further 10 minutes. Remove and serve.

INGREDIENTS

1 small onion
1 clove garlic
3 tablespoons olive oil
600 ml water
2 chopped peeled tomatoes
3 okras
3 ears baby corn
3 tablespoons cooked kidney beans
350 g sticky rice
salt and pepper to taste

SUGGESTION
Add three drops of Tabasco sauce to the rice.

Easy
45 minutes
4

Biological rice
with seaweed

Soak the seaweed in water. Chop the onion and stew in olive oil. Add the rice and the water; season with salt and pepper. Let cook and, if necessary, add a little more water. After 10 minutes, add the peppers cut into pieces, the broccoli stems and seaweed. Cook for 20 minutes more. Serve the rice with the tofu cheese, cut into cubes.

Vegetable tart
in the oven

Prepare the dough: Dilute the yeast in a little water; then mix it into the flour with the remaining water and a little salt. Stretch it out and leave to leaven for 30 minutes at room temperature. Roll it out over a floured surface and line a mould previously greased with butter and powdered with flour.

Cut the broccoli and leeks into pieces; cook in salted water. Stew the onion and garlic cloves in rounds in olive oil. Season with salt; let brown and add the vegetables; cook for five minutes. Place them on the dough.

Mix the eggs with the cream and add the nutmeg; season with salt and pepper. Cover the vegetables with this preparation and place in an oven set at 160° C for 30 minutes.

INGREDIENTS

Dough:
12 g bakers yeast
100 ml tepid water
500 g flour
salt, butter
and flour to taste

Filling:
300 g broccoli
2 leeks
50 ml olive oil
2 medium onions
4 cloves garlic
2 eggs
250 ml Soya cream
1 coffeespoon nutmeg
salt and pepper to taste

800 ml water
1 laurel leaf
4 cloves garlic
2 tablespoons tomato
concentrate
50 ml olive oil
1 small onion
2 tomatoes
350 g rice
100 g green beans
100 g cauliflower
100 g green asparagus
3 carrots
salt and pepper to taste

Vegetarian paella

Easy
30 minutes
4

Boil the water with the laurel, half of the chopped cloves of garlic, tomato concentrate, salt and pepper; set aside.

Stew the onion and the remaining chopped cloves of garlic in olive oil in a paella dish. Let brown and add the tomatoes, cut into cubes. Add the rice, mix and leave to cook a little longer.

Slice the green beans, cauliflower and the green asparagus into small pieces, and the carrots into rounds. Add to the rice and cover with the tomato sauce mixture prepared before cooking.

MAIN DISHES

Seitan steak with turnip greens

Arrange the greens and cook them in salted water; keep hot. Cut the seitan into steaks; season with sliced cloves of garlic, laurel leaf, white wine, Soya sauce, salt and pepper to taste.

Remove the seeds from the pepper and cut it into slices. Heat the olive oil and slowly cook the steaks. Pour in the melted margarine and add the pepper; let cook for 10 minutes. Adjust the seasoning and serve the steaks.

INGREDIENTS

2 bundles turnip greens
800 g seitan
3 cloves garlic
1 laurel leaf
50 ml white wine
1 orange pepper
50 ml olive oil
Soya sauce,
salt and pepper to taste

DIFFERENT
SEASONING
Mix 500 ml of water,
a tablespoon of rice
vinegar, Soya sauce
and a teaspoon
of flour in a bowl.
Add at the end,
mix well and leave
to thicken.

Vegetarian chop-suey

Easy
30 minutes
4

Soak the mushrooms in warm water and leave to soften; drain, cut into pieces and leave to one side. Arrange the onion, carrots, leek and bamboo. Cut all into fine slices and sauté with the Soya bean sprouts in a mixture of oils. Add the prepared mushrooms and mix well; season with salt, pepper and Soya sauce. Remove and serve hot.

MAIN DISHES

Soy nachos

Soak the nachos in Soya sauce until they soften; set aside. Boil the eggs in plenty of water for approximately 10 minutes; cool under running water, shell them, cut into sections and set aside.

Cook the potatoes, cut into pieces, in plenty of water; drain and set aside. Stew the onion in half moons and the chopped garlic in olive oil; season with salt and pepper.

Mix the drained nachos, sections of egg, potatoes and chopped coriander. Place in the oven, set at 160° C, for 20 minutes; if necessary add more olive oil, so there is no dehydration.

INGREDIENTS

100 g soy nachos
1 tablespoon Soya sauce
3 eggs
800 g potatoes
5 tablespoons olive oil
2 small onions
2 cloves garlic
1 sprig coriander
salt and pepper to taste

INGREDIENTS

2 cloves garlic
1 sprig coriander
1 teaspoon ginger
1 onion
1 natural yoghurt
300 g seitan
100 ml oil
1 teaspoon cumin seeds
1 teaspoon cloves
2 aniseed stars
1 stick cinnamon
300 g basmati rice
600 ml boiling water
salt and pepper to taste

Easy

30 minutes

4

Seitan with spices and basmati rice

Chop the cloves of garlic and coriander and mix them with the ginger. Cut the onion into half moons; stir all into the yoghurt and leave in the fridge. Cut the seitan into cubes and fry in half of the very hot oil.

Aside, mix the cumin, cloves, aniseed and cinnamon; season with salt and pepper. Add the yoghurt preparation and mix well; let simmer on low heat for 10 minutes.

Heat the remaining oil; add the rice and leave to fry a little. Add the water, season with salt and leave to cook for 12 minutes. Loosen the rice and serve it with the seitan.

Portuguese gnocchi

Stew the onion and the chopped garlic cloves in olive oil; leave to soak in and add the tomatoes, cut into small cubes; season with salt and pepper to taste. Add the gnocchi; mix well and leave to cook for five minutes.

Add a little water, Soya sauce and leave to cook for a few more minutes, stirring from time to time. Adjust the seasoning and serve the gnocchi sprinkled with chopped parsley.

INGREDIENTS

50 ml olive oil
1 small onion
2 cloves garlic
2 tomatoes
600 g fresh gnocchi
1 teaspoon Soya sauce
1 sprig chopped parsley
salt and pepper to taste

SUGGESTION

Chop a quarter of Soya chorizo into small pieces and add to the gnocchi.

INGREDIENTS

100 g baby corn
300 g okra
100 g baby carrots
200 g green beans
1 onion
3 cloves garlic
1/2 green pepper
50 ml olive oil
350 g rice
water, salt and pepper
to taste

SUGGESTION
Chop 30g ginger
and mix in stew.

Coloured paella

Easy

30 minutes

4

Cut corn and okra into pieces, and carrot and beans into slices; cook in salted water. Reserve 800 ml of the vegetable broth.

Chop onion, garlic cloves and pepper; stew in olive oil. Let thicken; then, add rice and mix well.

Stir onto the rice and cook for 15 minutes, adding remaining broth little by little. Remove the paella and serve.

Seitan kebabs

Cut the seitan into cubes; marinate with soy sauce. Mix with olive oil and chop aromatic herbs; set aside.

Make kebabs with seitan, alternating with green, red and orange peppers cut into pieces.

Grill, on low heat, together with tomatoes, cut in half.

Sprinkle, from time to time, with sesame oil. Serve kebabs with the tomato, seasoned with the reserved aromatic olive oil.

INGREDIENTS

500 g seitan
2 tablespoons soy sauce
1 green pepper
1 red pepper
1 orange pepper
50 ml olive oil
1 sprig chopped coriander
1 sprig chopped parsley
4 tomatoes
2 tablespoons
sesame oil
salt and pepper to taste

SUGGESTION
Add soy chorizo, cut
into pieces, to the
kebabs.

Dough:
750 g flour
7 teaspoons yeast

Sauce:
50 ml olive oil
3 small onions
2 cloves garlic
180 g peeled tomatoes
1 teaspoon sugar
100 ml white wine

Filling:
3 ripe tomatoes
100 g tofu
2 cloves garlic
100 ml soy drink
1 tablespoon pine kernels
salt, pepper, oregano,
basil and coriander
to taste

Tomato and pesto pizza

Easy
30 minutes
8

Mix flour with yeast and water, until a firm dough is formed; season with salt and let rest a while. Roll dough on a pizza base.

Prepare the tomato sauce, stewing an onion and half the garlic cloves in olive oil. Add the chopped tomatoes; season with salt, pepper and sugar. Bring to boil and add the wine. Let cook slowly; strain sauce and pour over pizza base.

Arrange tomatoes and onion rings on top. Mash the tofu with garlic cloves, soy drink, salt and pepper. Pour over pizza and sprinkle with pine nuts, oregano, basil and coriander, all chopped. Bake pizza at 220°C for 15 minutes.

Red cabbage pie

Set the oven at 160° C. Cut the red cabbage, green beans and the pepper into slices. Heat them in water, seasoned with salt and pepper. Heat the broccoli separately and chop them. Cook the potatoes separately and then reduce them to a purée. Season it will salt, pepper and nutmeg. Mix the broccoli into the purée and leave to one side.

Husk and chop the onion and the cloves of garlic. Stew them in olive oil and add the carrots, green beans, red cabbage and the green pepper. Mix all well and let stew a little.

Place a layer of the potato purée on a heat resistant tray, followed by one of the vegetables and end with another layer of purée. Brush the surface of the pie with beaten egg. Leave in the upper shelf of the oven to cook au gratin for 20 minutes.

INGREDIENTS

200 g red cabbage
200 g green beans
1 green pepper
100 g broccoli
800 g potato
1 small chopped onion
3 cloves of garlic
50 ml olive oil
3 grated carrots
2 eggs
salt, pepper
and nutmeg to taste

SUGGESTION

Add a quarter
of chopped soya
chorizo to the stew.

INGREDIENTS

6 decilitres boiling water
1 tablespoon of butter
250 g noodle dough
1.5 dl of olive oil
1 sprig of coriander
2 tablespoons of pine nuts
1 soup spoon of parmesan cheese
2 tomatoes
salt and pepper to taste

SUGGESTION

Replace the coriander with sweet basil.

Easy //
25 minutes
4 Y|

Noodles
with coriander pesto

Place the butter in the water. Place the noodles on a tray and pour in the water, mixed with the butter. Leave to rest for four minutes. Drain well.

Place the olive oil, coriander, pine nuts and the cheese in a mincer. Grind everything. Season with salt and pepper and mix this preparation with the noodles, folding in with care. Serve, garnished with tomatoes cut into sections.

Vegetarian pizza

Dissolve the yeast into water and add flour, previously seasoned with a pinch of salt, to it. Knead well. Cover with a cloth and leave to leaven, until the volume has doubled. Set the oven at 200° C.

Cut the onion into fine half moons, slice the mushrooms and cut the pepper into small cubes.

Roll the dough out over a floured surface. Line the pizza base with the dough. Spread the tomato pulp over the dough and superimpose the prepared vegetables, sweetcorn and olives, cut into rounds. Sprinkle with oregano and place on a middle shelf in the oven for 20 minutes.

INGREDIENTS

Dough:
7 g baker's yeast
300 g flour
1.5 dl of tepid water
salt to taste

Covering:
1 onion
100 g mushrooms
1 red pepper
150 g sweetcorn
80 g stoned black olives
1 dl of tomato pulp
1 tablespoon of oregano
flour to taste

INGREDIENTS

200 g granulated soya
1 kg potatoes
2 cloves of garlic
1 laurel leaf
1 tablespoon
of pepper paste
1 dl of white wine
1 tablespoon
of soya sauce
1 dl of olive oil
1 teaspoon of chopped
spring onion
oil, pickles
and olives to taste

Portuguese soya

Easy //
50 minutes
4

Soak the soya in cold water for an hour. Peel the potatoes, cut them into cubes and fry them in very hot oil. Leave to one side.

Drain the soya. Season it with the chopped cloves of garlic, laurel, pepper paste, wine and soya sauce. Leave to marinate for 30 minutes. Then drain the soya and fry it in the olive oil. Refresh with the liquid from the marinade and mix the fried potatoes in. Adjust the seasoning and add the chopped pickles and black olives. Sprinkle with spring onion and serve.

Vegetarian fricassee

Cut the vegetables into pieces. Chop two cloves of garlic. Stew them in half of the olive oil. Add the carrot, cauliflower, leek and half of the water. Season with salt and pepper. After five minutes, add the broccoli, courgette and pepper, leaving to cook. Remove and keept the vegetables and the cooking broth to one side.

Chop the remaining cloves of garlic and stew them in the left over olive oil. Add the rice, season with salt and mix in. Add the remaining water and cook for 12 minutes.

Melt the butter and add it to the flour. Add the cooking broth from the vegetables and mix. Add the vegetables, lemon juice, soya milk and egg yolks. Adjust the seasoning and serve with the rice.

INGREDIENTS

2 carrots
200 g cauliflower
1 leek
(white part)
200 g broccoli
1 courgette
1 red pepper
4 cloves of garlic
2 onions
1 dl of olive oil
8 dl of water
to boil
200 g rice
1 tablespoon
of margarine
1 tablespoon of flour
1 lemon (juice)
2 dl of soya milk
2 egg yolks
salt, pepper and parsley
to taste

Vegetarian meat balls

Easy
1 hour
4

Immerse the soya into the water and leave it to rest for 20 minutes. Peel the potatoes. Cook them in water with salt. Drain them and reduce to purée. Mix the two egg yolks, butter, hot milk, pepper and nutmeg in.

Chop the onion, cloves of garlic, pepper and parsley. Drain the soya well. Mix everything in. Add the egg and the remaining beaten egg yolk and mould the meat balls.

Cover with flour and fry them in hot oil. Drain them and place on a gentle heat with the tomato sauce. Adjust the seasoning and serve the meat balls with the potato purée.

Soya bean stew

Soak the beans the day before. Cook in water with a trickle of olive oil. Remove and also keep a little of the cooking water. Sink the soya in hot water and let rest for 20 minutes.

Stew the chopped cloves of garlic and onion in olive oil. Add the chopped, peeled and seedless tomatoes. Refresh with the wine.

Mix the drained soya and small cubed peppers. Season with soya sauce, some drops of sesame oil and ginger. Leave to stew for 12 minutes. When seven minutes run over, add the green beans, cut into slices, the azuki beans and the cooking water to finish. Leave to cook for eight minutes and serve.

INGREDIENTS

150 g azuki beans
250 g granulated soya
2 cloves of garlic
1 onion
50 ml olive oil
3 ripe tomatoes
1 dl of white wine
1/2 red peppers
1 tablespoon of soya sauce
1 teaspoon of grated ginger
150 g green beans
olive oil and sesame oil to taste

SUGGESTION

Add 20 grams of hijiki seaweed soaked for 10 minutes to the preparation.

INGREDIENTS

2 cloves of garlic
1 onion
50 ml sunflower oil
1 laurel leaf
2 ripe tomatoes
300 g turnip
300 g carrots
200 g green beans
400 g tofu
2 pieces of burnet
salt, pepper and grated
ginger to taste

SUGGESTION

Add 100 grams of soya
beansprouts to the
vegetarian mix.

Vegetarian mix

Easy
40 minutes
4

Chop the cloves of garlic and the onion. Stew them in sunflower oil and also the laurel. Add the chopped seedless tomatoes. Leave to stew.

Husk the turnip and peel the carrots. Cut them into small cubes.

Remove the ends from the green beens and cut them into pieces. Add the vegetables to the stew and also the tofu in cubes, and leave to cook for 15 minutes. Add the vegetables and a little water. Season with salt, pepper, burnet and a little grated ginger. Leave to finish cooking. Adjust the seasoning and serve.

Tofu with carrot rice

Cut the tofu into slices. Season it with powdered garlic, soya sauce and sesame oil. Leave to marinate for 15 minutes. Cover with wheat flour, beaten egg and cassava flour. Fry in hot oil and drain on absorbent paper. Leave to one side.

Stew the chopped onion in the olive oil. Add the rice and carrots, cut into cubes and leave to fry. Irrigate with boiling water and season with salt. Cook for 10 minutes. Serve the breaded tofu with the carrot rice. Garnish with parsley, lemon sections and ketchup.

INGREDIENTS

600 g tofu
1 teaspoon of powdered garlic
2 tablespoons of soya sauce
1 coffee spoon of sesame oil
1 onion
50 ml olive oil
300 g rice
2 carrots
6 dl of water
Wheat flour, eggs, cassava flour, oil, salt, parsley, lemon and ketchup to taste

SUGGESTION

Substitute the cassava flour with maize semolina, or grated bread (breadcrumbs) mixed with aromatic herbs.

INGREDIENTS

300 g broccoli
1 dl of olive oil
1 small onion
2 cloves of garlic
200 g carrots
200 g of long tapered
or sticky rice
4 tablespoons of grated
parmesan cheese
salt and pepper to taste

Oven rice

Easy //
30 minutes
4

Separate the broccoli into bunches and cook them in plenty of water, seasoned with half of the olive oil, salt and pepper. Remove and keep the vegetable and the cooking water. Set the oven at 180° C.

Husk and chop the onion, cloves of garlic and the carrots. Stew them in the remaining olive oil and add the rice. Blend well and

water with five decilitres of the prepared broth. Cover the pan and leave to cook on a gentle heat for 10 minutes. Mix in the broccoli and remove.

Place the rice on a tray and sprinkle with the parmesan cheese. Leave on the middle shelf of the oven for 10 minutes.

Vegan rice pudding

Boil the water with lemon rinds, a cinnamon stick and a pinch of salt. Add margarine and rice when it starts boiling, wash and drain. Let cook until rice "opens".

Aside, put soy drinks and rice on stove; when it begins to boil, pour the mixture over the rice and let simmer, on low heat, stirring continuously. Then add yellow sugar and cook until creamy.

Remove lemon rinds and cinnamon stick; Let cool a little and place into bowls. Sprinkle with cinnamon and serve cold.

INGREDIENTS

600 ml water
2 lemon rinds
1 stick cinnamon
1 teaspoon vegetable
margarine
150 g rice
1 l soya drink
200 ml rice drink
120 g yellow sugar
salt and cinnamon
powder to taste

SUGGESTION
So that the rice pudding
has more colour, mix
in a teaspoon of
custard powder
5 minutes before
removing from heat.

Papaya cream

Easy /|

30 minutes

4 🍴

Mix a little rice milk with custard and three tablespoons brown sugar. Add cinnamon, aniseed, lemon rind, remaining milk and cook on low heat, stirring continuously until thickened. Let cool, stirring from time to time; set aside.

Blend the papaya with the sugar and place into cups, alternating with the previous mixture. End with the cream, and sprinkle with the cinnamon powder and toasted almonds. Serve chilled.

Banana and pineapple ice cream

Easy

15 minutes

4

Blend well one banana with two pineapple rounds, yoghurt, soy drink and corn jam.

Cut remaining banana into rounds, pineapple into small pieces and strawberries into quarters. Place fruits into cups and sprinkle with cinnamon.

Place beaten mixture into ice cube trays and refrigerate, until frozen. Then, turn out of moulds and place into cups.

INGREDIENTS

2 bananas
3 pineapple rounds
2 natural soya yoghurts
50 ml soya drink
2 tablespoons corn jam
4 strawberries
cinnamon to taste

SUGGESTION
Add 100 grams of strawberries to ingredients to blend.

300 g dried figs
400 g tofu
4 tablespoons carob
bean flour
1 teaspoon vanilla
essence
sliced almonds
and fresh figs to taste

Fig mousse

Easy ⚔️
25 minutes 🕐
4 🍴

Soak dried figs in water and let rest for 2 hours. Then, drain and reduce to purée.

Add the tofu, carob bean flour and vanilla; mash until a mousse is formed. Place into small cups and decorate with chopped almonds and fresh figs. Serve dessert cold.

Bean carob pancakes

Add the three types of flour to the yeast, water, tofu cream, sunflower oil and corn jam. Mix really well until homogenised; let rest for a few minutes.

Place a non-stick frying pan on the stove and brush with sunflower oil. Put in a portion of dough and allow to cook on both sides; remove and repeat until the dough is finished.

Group some of the pancakes and sprinkle with cocoa and grated vegan chocolate. Decorate to taste.

INGREDIENTS

40 g carob bean flour
80 g wheat flour
1 teaspoon of corn
starch
1 teaspoon yeast powder
150 ml water
80 g tofu cream
50 ml sunflower oil
1 tablespoon corn jam
sunflower oil, cocoa
and vegan chocolate
to taste

SUGGESTION
Cover the pancakes
with previously softened
soya vanilla ice cream.

INGREDIENTS

200 ml vegetable cream
100 g tofu cream cheese
2 tablespoons yellow
sugar
50 ml lemon juice
4 large ready made
tartlets
200 g strawberries

SUGGESTION
Cover with melted
organic chocolate.

Easy

1 hour

4

Strawberry
and tofu tartlets

Beat the cream and mix it with the tofu cream cheese. Add the sugar and lemon juice. Pour the preparation into the tartlets.

Reduce the strawberries to a purée and pour onto the previously prepared cream. Serve the tartlets cold, decorated to taste.

Carrot tart

Peel the carrots and cut them into pieces; cook in water, seasoned with a pinch of salt; drain and reduce to a purée. Grease a baking tray with margarine and line it with greased wax paper; set aside. Turn on the oven to 180º C.

Mash the tofu and add the carrot purée; then add the sugar and flour. Beat the egg whites to a stiff peak and fold into the preparation. Flavour with orange rind and pour the mixture onto the baking tray. Leave in the oven for 25 minutes.

Remove and leave to cool a little; turn out of the mould onto a cooking cloth, sprinkled with a little sugar. Cover the cake with marmalade. Curl up in the shape of a tart and keep in the fridge until it becomes well chilled. Serve sprinkled with cinnamon powder and orange rind.

INGREDIENTS

500 g carrots
160 g tofu
220 g yellow sugar
100 g flour
4 egg whites
1 orange rind
1 teacup stewed organic
marmalade
salt, vegetable margarine
and cinnamon to taste

SUGGESTION
Chop 50 grams
of walnut kernels
and fold them into the
mixture, before
pouring onto
the baking tray.

INGREDIENTS

6 apples
1 lemon (juice)
8 tablespoons soya milk
50 g vegetable margarine
150 g yellow sugar
1 teaspoon anise
1 tablespoon ale yeast
100 g walnut kernels
250 g flour
1 teaspoon powdered yeast
vegetable butter and flour to taste

Apple and walnut cake

Easy
1 hour
12

Heat the oven at 180° C. Grease a 22 cm round cake tin with butter and flour it; set aside. Peel the apples and cut them in half; take out the pips with incisions and sprinkle with lemon juice; set aside.

Beat the egg yolks really well with the margarine and sugar until a cream is formed. Mix the anise with the ale yeast and add it to the egg yolk cream. Mix in the walnut kernels in flour, as well as the yeast and add it to the previous preparation. Finally, beat the egg whites to stiff peaks and fold into the mixture. Pour into the cake tin and put the apples on top. Leave in the oven for 45 minutes. Remove from the oven, turn out of the tin and serve.

Tofu croquettes

30 minutes

18

Grease a baking tray with butter and line it with greased wax paper. Set the oven at 180° C.

Beat the butter with the sugar; add the egg, tofu, a little grated lemon and the chopped walnuts. Blend all really well and sprinkle with the cinnamon and flour. Mix a little more and leave the mixture to rest for five minutes.

Remove small quantities of the mixture using a teaspoon and arrange them spaced out on the baking tray. Place in the oven for 10 to 12 minutes. Remove the croquettes from the oven and, aided by a spatula, release them. Serve warm or cold.

INGREDIENTS

50 g vegetable butter
150 g yellow sugar
1 egg
50 g tofu
40 g chopped walnuts
1 teaspoon powdered
cinnamon
150 g whole flour
vegetable butter
and grated lemon
to taste

SUGGESTION
Fill the croquettes with
sweet red fruits sauce.

INGREDIENTS

3 rounds fresh pineapple
3 tablespoons brown
sugar
100 g tofu
2 two peach soya
yoghurts
red fruits to taste

SUGGESTION
Add a little
grated tangerine to the
yoghurt cream.

Creamy pineapple

Easy
30 minutes
4

Cut the pineapple into cubes and add the sugar. Place on the stove and cook for a few minutes; remove and let cool.

Mix the tofu with the yoghurt in a container and stir well; set aside. Place the sweet pineapple sauce in the bottom of cups and top with tofu cream. Decorate with red fruits and serve.

Tofu pudding

Soak the gelatine sheets in cold water. Mix the sugar with the custard powder. Add the soya drink and place on the stove together with the tofu; leave to thicken and remove.

Drain the gelatine and mix well into the previous preparation. Grease some small moulds with oil and pour in. Leave to cool and take the puddings out of the moulds. Decorate with red fruits.

INGREDIENTS

5 sheets clear gelatine
100 g yellow sugar
3 tablespoons custard powder
500 ml vanilla soya drink
50 g tofu
oil and red fruits to taste

SUGGESTION

Add two tablespoons of toasted and crushed almond kernels.

INGREDIENTS

6 sheets of clear gelatine
500 ml soya drink
3 tablespoons custard cream
200 g yellow sugar
2 thin rinds lemon
1 stick cinnamon
80 g tofu cream
200 ml soya cream
13 wholemeal cocoa biscuits
coffee and crushed biscuits to taste

CRUNCHY
Add two tablespoons of chopped walnuts to the cream.

Tofu pave

Easy

45 minutes

4

Soak the gelatine sheets in cold water. Heat the soya drink until it becomes warm; add the custard cream, sugar, thin lemon rinds and the cinnamon stick. Heat until it thickens. Remove and take out the lemon rind and cinnamon stick.

Add the drained sheets of gelatine to the preparation, then heat, stirring until it dissolves. Also add the tofu cream; leave to cool.

Beat the cream and mix it into the cold cream. Line a rectangular cake tin, English cake style, with cling film.

Dip the biscuits in coffee; arrange half at the bottom of the cake tin and spread half of the tofu cream on top; repeat this operation again, ending with the biscuits. Place in the fridge to solidify. Turn out of the tin and sprinkle with ground biscuits. Serve.

Tofu cheesecake

Grease a flan dish, with a movable base, with butter. Mix the butter with the biscuits and almond, until it forms a rich paste. Place the preparation on the bottom of the mould, pressing with the hands.

To prepare the cream: Boil three quarters of the soya milk and add the nigari. While curdling, strain through a fine cloth, obtaining tofu. Boil the remaining milk and half of the sugar and the vanilla. Beat the still hot milk with the tofu and remaining sugar in a blender. Pour over the flan dish and place in the fridge to solidify. Remove, turn out of the mould and serve, decorated to taste.

INGREDIENTS

50 g vegetable butter
100 g ground Marie biscuits
100 g ground almond
vegetable butter to taste

Cream:
2 litres soya milk
2 tablespoons nigari
100 g sugar
1/2 vanilla pod

NIGARI

It is a Japanese product, used as a tofu coagulant.
It is formed of magnesium chloride, obtained from sea water, via a process which gives nigari crystals.

4 kiwis
4 soya yoghurts
4 crepes
icing sugar to taste

SUGGESTION
Before adding the soya
yoghurts, mix
a spoonful
of breakfast cereal
into them.

Soya and kiwi cream

Easy
10 minutes
4

Peel the kiwis; cut them into cubes and distribute half into cups. Pour the yoghurts in and place the remaining kiwi on top. Leave in the fridge.

When serving the dessert, cut the crepes into fine slices and place them in the cups. Sprinkle with icing sugar and decorate to taste.

Cheese mousse with forest fruits

Put a pan on the stove with 100 grams of fruit, the wine, sugar and sticks of cinnamon. Let boil until the wine is reduced and the fruit becomes soft with a caramelised appearance.

Mousse preparation: Whisk the cream and set aside. Place the fresh cheese in a bowl and knead it to obtain a paste. Add the whisked cream and mix well. Place the mousse in the fridge to make it a little more solid.

Remove the stewed fruit from the heat and let cool a while in the fridge. Distribute the mousse into cups, add the stewed forest fruits and decorate with the remaining fruit and mint.

INGREDIENTS

150 g forest fruits
50 ml red wine
50 g sugar
2 sticks cinnamon
2 tablespoons soya cream
250 g fresh cheese

INGREDIENTS

1 tablespoon lemon agar-agar seaweed (grated)
500 ml vanilla soya drink
2 tablespoons fructose
4 tablespoons flour
1 lemon (grated)
6 rounds of tinned pineapple
200 ml soya cream
8 apple flavoured wholemeal biscuits
200 ml water to boil
1 tablespoon pomegranate juice
pineapple and myrtle to taste

Pineapple cream

Easy
40 minutes
8

Add a tablespoon of agar-agar seaweed to three tablespoons of soya drink; set aside. Mix the fructose with the flour and dissolve in a little of the same drink. Boil the rest and pour hot over the previous mixture. Add the grated lemon and previously prepared agar-agar. Place on the stove to thicken, stirring continuously. Remove from the heat and let cool.

Add half of the chopped pineapple and whisked cream. Place a little crushed biscuit in the bottom of cups and pour the cream on top, without totally filling them. Leave in the fridge until solid. Cut the remaining pineapple into triangles and arrange over the cups, along with some myrtles. Again leave in the fridge.

Soak a little of the agar-agar seaweed (approximately a teaspoon) in a little water for five minutes, and then mix in boiling water and add the pomegranate juice. Let cool and pour into the cups. Place in the fridge again to solidify. Serve very cold.

Mango filled biscuits

Soak the agar-agar seaweed in water. Place on a gentle heat with the mango pulp for 10 minutes. Remove and let cool. Beat the cream; add granulated sugar and beat for a little longer, until completely dissolved. Blend in the mango pulp preparation.

Pour the cream into a rectangular container, lined with cling film, and place in the freezer to solidify. Take the preparation out of the mould and, with a round cutter, cut the mango preparation. Fill the biscuits two by two. Serve them, decorated with melted chocolate.

INGREDIENTS

1 tablespoon agar-agar
seaweed
50 ml water
200 ml mango pulp
200 ml vegetal cream
50 g icing sugar
8 sugar free
apple and
cinnamon biscuits
melted chocolate
to taste

TO MAKE STRONGER
Add grated lemon
to the mango preparation
or 50 ml of vodka.

Fresh tropical sweet

Easy

30 minutes

10

Soak the agar-agar seaweed in water for 10 minutes. Boil the juice with three tablespoons of fructose and the seaweed for 10 minutes. Then, remove and let cool a little. Peel and slice the mango.

Grease a 20 x 15 cm Pyrex dish with oil and arrange the mango in layers. Add the juice and fructose preparation and leave in the fridge to solidify.

Remove and with a cutter, cut into circles. Whisk the cream with the remaining fructose; place in a pastry-cook bag and decorate the gelatine rounds with a chantilly rosette. Sprinkle with cocoa and serve cold.

Peach cup

Soak the agar-agar seaweed in cold water. Peel the peaches; Remove the stones and cut into small cubes. Boil the fructose with the water, seaweed, cinnamon and peaches for 10 minutes. Reduce to purée and let cool.

Whisk the cream; add the condensed milk and a third of the peach purée. Distribute a little of the purée in the base of cups, and then the cream. Melt 100 grams of cooking chocolate in a bain marie; pour it over the cream; add another layer of purée and to finish, the remaining cream. Keep in the fridge. Serve decorated to taste.

INGREDIENTS

1 teaspoon agar-agar seaweed
2 peaches
3 tablespoons fructose
200 ml water
1 cinnamon stick
400 ml vegetable cream
100 ml condensed milk
100 g bar chocolate

INGREDIENTS

4 eggs
50 g sugar
1 tablespoon flour
2 tablespoons cocoa powder
1 tablespoon agar-agar seaweed
300 ml water
50 ml blackcurrant syrup
200 ml vegetable cream
50 g icing sugar
100 g cream cheese
100 g red fruits
butter and sugar to taste

Easy //
1 hour 🕐
8 🍴

Cheese and red fruit delight

Set the oven at 180° C. Grease a 20 x 30 cm baking tray with butter and line it with greased wax paper. Whisk the eggs with the sugar until the volume has doubled. Fold in the flour and cocoa; blend and pour onto the tray. Place in the oven for 15 minutes.

Soak the agar-agar in water for 10 minutes then boil for five. Keep a third aside; add the blackcurrant syrup. Whisk the cream with the sugar and cream cheese. Pour in the reserved seaweed water and mix well.

Turn the cake out of the mould onto a surface sprinkled with icing sugar. Cut into quarters, assisted by a 10 cm diameter cutting ring. Place the cake on the base of the ring and add the cream.

Arrange the red fruits on top and leave in the fridge to solidify. Remove and add the blackcurrant sauce. Again, leave in the fridge to solidify. Take out of the mould and cut each quarter into triangles.

Chocolate pudding

Easy
1 hour
4

Soak the agar-agar seaweed in water for 10 minutes. Place on the stove and cook for five minutes; remove and let cool. Heat the milk and set aside.

Split the chocolate into pieces and melt in a bain marie. Mix a half with a third of the water with seaweed and milk. Line small cutting rings with cling film and grease them with oil.

Distribute the chocolate preparation in the rings and place them in the fridge to solidify. Whisk the cream and add it to the remaining water, condensed milk and the other half of the chocolate. Pour this cream into the rings and leave in the freezer until solid. Take out of the mould and decorate to taste.

INGREDIENTS

1 tablespoon agar-agar
seaweed
200 ml water
100 ml milk
200 g cooking chocolate
200 ml vegetable cream
100 ml condensed milk
50 g shelled and ground
toasted almonds
oil to taste

SUGGESTION
Cover the puddings
with melted chocolate
and decorate with
red fruits.

INGREDIENTS

1 teaspoon of
agar-agar seaweed
3 tablespoons of brown
sugar
3 tablespoons of cream
custard
400 ml milk
1 packet of pie dough
4 tinned pear halves
vegetable butter,
flour, beaten egg
and icing sugar to taste

Pear delight

Easy
1 hour
10

Soak the agar-agar seaweed in cold water for eight minutes; heat on the stove for five minutes. Apart, dissolve the sugar and cream custard in the milk and heat until it thickens. Add the seaweed and let cook a little longer. Remove and let the cream cool; set aside.

Set the oven at 180° C. Grease a baking tray with butter and sprinkle it with flour. Cut the pie dough into two portions, giving them a pear shape; arrange on the baking tray. Brush them with

beaten egg and place in the oven for 10 minutes.

Coat the pears in syrup, sprinkle with icing sugar and place on the top shelf of the oven to cook au gratin. Remove the dough from the oven and distribute the cream over one of the portions; overlay with the au gratin pear slices and the other portion of the dough over them. Decorate with a little pear au gratin and sprinkle with icing sugar.

Plum delight

Boil half of the sugar with 300 ml of water. Add the plums and cook until a translucent syrup is obtained. Soak the agar-agar seaweed in the remaining cold water for 10 minutes. Then put it on the stove and let boil for five minutes. Add half of the stewed plum preparation and keep the other half aside.

Whisk the cream and mix in the cream cheese, remaining sugar and the reserved agar-agar seaweed preparation. Pour in the orange liqueur and mix. Distribute the stewed red plum into cups until half full; then, add the cream preparation and finish with a little more stewed fruit. Serve chilled, decorated to taste.

INGREDIENTS

150 g sugar
500 ml water
4 red plums
2 teaspoons agar-agar seaweed
200 ml vegetable cream
2 tablespoons cream cheese
1 tablespoon orange liqueur

INGREDIENTS

1 tablespoon agar-agar
200 ml water
1 teaspoon instant
coffee
300 ml vegetable cream
300 ml condensed milk
chantilly and vanilla
sticks to taste

Mocha ice cream

Easy

30 minutes

4

Soak the agar-agar seaweed in water for five minutes. Then put on the stove and let boil for five minutes. Add the instant coffee, remove from the heat and set aside.

Whisk the cream; add the condensed milk and mix in the coffee preparation. Mix and put in the freezer for six hours. When serving, make various ice cream balls and distribute them into cups. Decorate with chantilly and vanilla sticks.

SWEETS

Yoghurt cheesecake

Soak the agar-agar seaweed in a little cold water for 10 minutes. Then put on the stove and cook for five minutes. Whisk the cream and add the yoghurt, cream cheese and corn jam. Mix everything really well and add the still hot seaweed preparation.

Put a ring on a serving dish and place the cake base, with the same diameter as the ring, on it. Pour on the reserved cream and put in the freezer to solidify. Prepare the gelatine, following the instructions on the packet.

Peel and cut the kiwis into rounds. Place them on the cream and the gelatine over them. Again, put in the freezer for 40 minutes. Remove the ring and serve cold.

INGREDIENTS

2 tablespoons
agar-agar seaweed
200 ml vegetable cream
1 red fruits yoghurt
2 tablespoons
cream cheese
2 tablespoons
corn jam
1 cake base
500 ml all fruit gelatine
2 kiwis

Apple pastries

Easy
1 hour and 30 minutes
12

Add to the flour the butter and a pinch of salt. Mix well and add the soya drink gradually. Mix well and leave to rest for 15 minutes in the fridge. Set the oven at 180° C.

Peel the apples and remove the seeds. Cut them into fine strips and cover with lemon juice; set aside. Roll out the dough until it becomes fine and cut it into circles; place two or three apple slices in the centre of each one and sprinkle with a little yellow sugar.

Brush the edges with a little water and join them to form pastries. Place them on a baking tray lightly powdered with flour. Heat the corn jam with the water and brush the pastries with the same. Sprinkle with sesame seeds and place in the oven for approximately 25 minutes. Serve warm or cold.

Banana pancakes

Mix the flour with the bran, seedless raisins and soya drink. Mix well. Add the crushed banana and mix. Grease a small non-stick frying pan with soya butter; heat a little and add a scoop of cream.

Leave to become golden on both sides. Spread the pancakes with corn jam and serve with fresh fruit to taste.

INGREDIENTS

190 g wheat flour
35 g wheat bran
30 g raisins
300 ml soya drink
1 banana
soya butter,
corn jam
and fresh fruit to taste

SUGGESTION
Serve the pancakes
with soya yoghurt
and fruit.

INGREDIENTS

2 eggs
100 g brown sugar
100 ml oil
200 ml soya milk
250 g flour
1 teaspoon powdered yeast
1 tablespoon cocoa
30 g chopped walnuts
vegetable butter
and corn jam to taste

Walnut cake

Easy

1 hour and 30 minutes

6

Beat the eggs with the brown sugar. Add the oil, milk and flour mixed with the yeast and cocoa. Blend everything really well and add half of the chopped walnuts.

Grease a round mould, with a lid, with the butter and then sprin-kle it with flour. Pour the mixture into the mould and put the re-maining walnuts on top.

Cover and steam for an hour and 15 minutes. Leave to cool, re-move and turn out of the mould. Spread with corn jam and serve.

Chocolate
and cereal fingers

Melt the two types of chocolate separately in a bain marie. Then, pour the vegan chocolate into rectangular silicon moulds and sprinkle with cereal flakes. Spread with melted white chocolate and sprinkle again with cereal flakes. Finish by distributing raspberries over the top. Put in the freezer to solidify and serve, cut into very cold fingers.

INGREDIENTS

200 g vegan chocolate
50 g white chocolate
50 g wheat cereal flakes
cereal flakes
and fresh raspberries
to taste

2 tablespoons custard powder
500 ml soya drink
1 stick cinnamon
2 lemon rinds
4 gelatine sheets
2 tablespoons fructose
200 ml vegetable cream
100 g whole-wheat biscuits
soya drink, forest fruits and cinnamon powder to taste.

Biscuit delight

Easy //
40 minutes
6

Blend the custard with the soya drink; mix well and add the cinnamon stick and lemon rind. Place the preparation on the stove until it thickens. Immerse the gelatine in cold water.

Remove the preparation from the heat; add the fructose and drained gelatine; mix all thoroughly. Remove the cinnamon stick and lemon rind; mix until cool and then blend in half of the whisked cream.

Place an acetate film in a ring and pour in a little of the cream. Grind the biscuits in soya drink and make alternate layers with the cream. Put in the fridge to solidify. Turn out of the mould, decorate with the remaining cream, forest fruits and cinnamon powder. Serve cold.

Fruit delight

Soak the gelatine sheets in cold water. Mix the cream custard with the milk, stirring continuously. Add the soya cream and place it on the stove to thicken. Remove and set aside. Drain the gelatine and add it to this preparation, as well as the sweetener; leave to cool. Whisk the vegetable cream and also fold into the cream.

Cook the fruits and jam in water; leave to cool. Grease a rectangular mould with a little oil and pour in the cream and the fruits. Place in the freezer until it becomes really firm; remove and take out of the mould. Decorate with cherry sauce, blackcurrants and mint and sprinkle with chocolate powder.

INGREDIENTS

7 sheets clear gelatine
3 tablespoons
cream custard
300 ml semi-skimmed
milk
200 ml soya cream
3 tablespoons
sweetener
200 ml vegetable cream
25 g myrtles
25 g blackcurrants
1 tablespoon jam
100 ml water
2 tablespoons
sugar free
cherry sauce
blackcurrants, mint
and fine chocolate
powder to taste

INGREDIENTS

4 apples
3 tablespoons corn jam
500 ml semi-skimmed milk
2 tablespoons ready made custard
1 aniseed star
1 stick cinnamon
2 lemon rinds
2 tablespoons fructose
200 ml soya cream

Easy

30 minutes

4

Creamy apples

Peel the apples, add the jam and simmer gently; remove and set aside.

Mix the milk with the prepared custard. Also add the aniseed, cinnamon stick and lemon rind; let thicken over a gentle heat. Remove from the heat and add the fructose. Remove the lemon rinds, aniseed and leave to cool.

Whisk the cream and add it to the previous preparation, blending in delicately. Place a little apple sauce in the base of cups and pour the cream on top. Decorate with the remaining apple, chill in the fridge and serve.

Chocolate biscuit cake

Mix the soya milk with the rice jam and corn starch. Place on the stove, stirring continuously, until it begins to thicken; then remove from the heat.

Place a layer of the cream preparation in a mould, followed by another of Marie biscuits. Continue to make layers until there are no more ingredients. Let cool and place in the freezer to solidify. Turn the cake out of the mould and sprinkle with grated chocolate. Serve cut into slices.

INGREDIENTS

1 litre chocolate
soya milk
8 tablespoons rice jam
3 tablespoons corn
starch
150 g Marie biscuits
grated chocolate
to taste

INGREDIENTS

60 ml soya drink
1 lemon rind
1 tablespoon
custard powder
5 tablespoons
sugar
1 cinnamon stick
100 g vegetable margarine
4 tablespoons
milk
1 tablespoon
lemon juice
3 tablespoons
flour
1 teaspoon
powdered yeast
8 kiwis
vegetable margarine
and flour to taste

Kiwi tarts

Easy

1 hour

4

Set the oven at 180° C. Prepare the cream custard: Place 40 ml of soya drink on the stove with the lemon rind and leave to boil. Mix well the custard powder with three tablespoons of sugar and the rest of the soya drink, a stick of cinnamon and 50 grams of margarine. Pour in the hot drink and put on the stove, stirring until it thickens. Remove from the heat and strain through a fine sieve; leave to cool, stirring occasionally.

Grease small tartlet moulds with vegetable margarine and flour them. Mix well the remaining sugar with the milk and the lemon juice. Add the remaining margarine, melted. Mix in the flour and yeast and distribute the preparation into the moulds. Place them in a heated oven and cook for 25 minutes.

Remove from the heat and let cool. Take out of the moulds, distribute the cream custard into the tartlets and place in the fridge. Peel the kiwis and cut them into half moons. Cover the cream with the fruit and serve the tartlets very cold.

Pineapple and mango delight

Set the oven at 180° C. Grease a round mould, 20 cm in diameter, with vegetable butter and sprinkle with flour. Melt the soya butter. Beat the eggs separately with the fructose; add the melted butter and continue to beat. Mix the yeast with the flour and add to the preparation. Pour into the mould and put in the oven to cook for 15 minutes. Remove and leave to cool.

Soak the gelatine sheets in cold water. Beat the cream. Add the yoghurts and the sweetener; mix and fold in half of the stewed fruit.

Drain the gelatine sheets and add three tablespoons of the previous preparation. Simmer gently until the gelatine sheets melt. Remove from the heat and add the rest of the cream; set aside.

Turn the cake out of the mould and cut with the help of a ring. Place the ring with the cake over a serving plate and cover it with cream. Smooth the surface and place in the freezer until solid. Decorate with the remaining stewed fruit and carefully remove the ring when serving. Serve well chilled.

INGREDIENTS

120 g soya butter
2 eggs
4 tablespoons
fructose
1 coffeespoon
powdered yeast
6 tablespoons
flour
10 clear gelatine sheets
500 ml vegetable cream
2 pineapple soya
yoghurts
1 tablespoon
sweetener
280 g sugar free
mango stewed fruit
vegetable butter
and flour to taste

INGREDIENTS

200 g wholegrain flour
1 packet instant yeast
100 ml warm soya milk
1 orange (rind and juice)
200 g pumpkin sauce
100 g flour
flour, corn jam
and cinnamon powder to
taste

Vegan pumpkin easter cake

Easy
1 hour
12

Mix 100 grams of whole flour with the yeast and half of the warm milk, until a homogenous dough is obtained. Add the rest of the milk and the whole flour, normal flour and orange peel and juice. Knead very well until a homogenous dough is obtained. Leave to rise for 25 minutes. Set the oven at 180° C.

Roll out the dough over a floured surface. Spread the pumpkin sauce over it, sprinkle with cinnamon powder and roll out. Leave to rise for a further 25 minutes. Make cuts in the top of the cake and place in the oven for 35 minutes. After it has cooked, leave to cool a little and brush with corn jam. Serve cut in slices.

Lemon charlotte

Run a cheesecake ring under water and line it with cling film. Soak the agar-agar seaweed. Mix the sugar with the custard powder separately. Add a trickle of milk, stirring continuously, until it dissolves. Add the lemon rind and agar-agar. Place on the stove and leave to simmer gently for five minutes, stirring constantly. Leave to cool.

Divide the rice cakes in half and line the cheesecake ring with them. Fill it with the cream preparation and place in the freezer to solidify. Beat the cream and decorate the charlotte, with the help of a pastry-cook's bag. Sprinkle with cocoa powder and serve cold.

INGREDIENTS

1 tablespoon agar-agar seaweed
100 g dark brown sugar
1 tablespoon custard powder
600 ml soya milk
1 lemon rind
5 whole rice cakes
200 ml vegetable cream
cocoa powder to taste

INGREDIENTS

100 g whole-wheat
biscuits
2 tablespoons
brown sugar
50 g raisins
50 g vegetable margarine
1 teaspoon cornstarch
1 tablespoon custard
powder
400 ml Soya drink
200 ml tangerine juice
vegetable margarine
to taste

Tangerine tartlets

Easy

1 hour

4

Grease small tartlet moulds with vegetable margarine and set aside. Set the oven at 180° C. Divide the biscuits into pieces and add the brown sugar, raisins and margarine; grind everything. Line the moulds with the mixture obtained and place in the oven for 10 minutes; remove and let cool.

Mix the cornstarch with the custard. Add the Soya drink and tangerine juice; mix. Put on low heat stirring continuously until a homogenous mixture is obtained.

Remove from the heat and leave to cool, stirring occasionally. Fill the tartlets with the tangerine preparation and put in the freezer to solidify a little. Serve decorated to taste.

Coconut cream

Mix the coconut milk with the Soya drink. Add the brown sugar and lemon rinds. Put on the stove and simmer gently, stirring continuously until it thickens. Leave to cool, stirring occasionally.

Distribute the preparation into cups and place in the fridge. Serve the coconut cream very cold, decorated with grated toasted coconut and blackcurrants.

INGREDIENTS

1 small bottle coconut
milk
200 ml Soya drink
2 lemon rinds
50 g brown sugar
grated toasted coconut
and blackcurrants
to taste

Easy
1 hour
4

Chocolate pineapple delight

Grease small cheesecake rings with Soya oil. Soak the agar-agar seaweed in 50 ml of cold water. Cut the pineapple into small cubes; place them, the fructose and the soaked seaweed in the remaining water on low heat. Let boil for five minutes; remove from the heat and reduce to a purée; strain through a net strainer.

Beat the cream; mix in the yoghurt and fold both into the pineapple preparation. Fill the rings with the cream obtained and place in the freezer until they solidify. Take out of the moulds and spread with the chocolate, previously melted in a bain marie. Decorate with fresh pineapple.

Mango pave with organic chocolate

Line a rectangular mould with cling film. Soak the agar-agar seaweed in water. Mix with the mango pulp and cook, boil for two minutes, stirring continuously. Remove from the heat and leave to cool completely.

Beat 300 ml of cream; fold it with the fructose into the previous mixture. Pour this cream into the mould in layers, alternating with whole biscuits, making the last layer biscuit.

Put in the freezer to solidify. At time of serving, turn the pave out of the mould and decorate with the remaining beaten cream, sweetened to taste, chocolate melted in bain marie and slices of mango.

INGREDIENTS

1 tablespoon
agar-agar seaweed
200 ml water
300 ml mango pulp
400 ml vegetal cream
1 tablespoon fructose
100 g wholemeal almond
biscuits
50 g bar organic
chocolate
sliced mango to taste

INGREDIENTS

800 ml Soya drink
200 g wild berries
1 tablespoon agar-agar seaweed
250 g sugar
200 ml vegetable cream
300 g biscuits
75 g vegetable butter
wild berries to taste

SUGGESTION
Add 100 grams of crushed almonds to the biscuits.

Wild berry ice

Easy //
30 minutes ⌐
10 🍴

Line a pan with waxed paper. Boil the Soya drink with the wild berries, agar-agar seaweed and sugar. Aside, beat the cream until smooth; fold in remaining preparation. Let cool and set aside.

Mix the ground biscuits with butter and line the base of the pan. Pour in the fruit preparation and refrigerate, until solid. Turn the ice-cake out of the mould carefully. Serve decorated with wild berries.

Strawberry cubes

Easy

30 minutes

4

Boil the water with the sugar and agar-agar seaweed; let dissolve and cool a little. Then place the strawberries, cut into halves, into ice trays. Fill with the previous preparation.

Refrigerate until completely solidified; remove the trays carefully and serve decorated to taste.

INGREDIENTS

1 l water
200 g sugar
1 tablespoon
agar-agar seaweed
200 g strawberries

SUGGESTION
Add a little
lemon juice
to the syrup.

1 l Soya drink
1/2 lemon (rind)
20 g ginger
250 g sugar
mint and sugar to taste

OPTION
Replace Soya drink
by another with
wild berry and vanilla
flavour.

Easy //
30 minutes 🕐
4 🍴

Lemon and ginger ice

Boil the Soya drink with the lemon rind and sliced ginger, leaving a little for decoration. Add the sugar; let boil and then wait until cool. Strain the mixture and pour into individual containers. Put in the freezer for one hour and 30 minutes.

Blend in a blender. Place in the freezer again for one hour. Repeat the operation until the ice cream reaches the desired consistency. Serve into cups, decorate with the remaining ginger and sprinkled sugar.

Gypsy cake

Turn on the oven at 180°C. Line a mould with waxed paper. Mash the tofu and mix well with the remaining ingredients, forming a stiff paste.

Pour mixture into a mould and bake for one hour and 30 minutes. Remove and let cool. Turn the cake out of the mould and sprinkle with icing sugar.

INGREDIENTS

100 g tofu
250 g brown sugar
250 g crushed almonds
100 g chocolate powder
400 pumpkin sweet
icing sugar to taste

SUGGESTION
Mix four tablespoons
of sliced almonds into
the paste.

INGREDIENTS

150 g vegetable butter
100 g brown sugar
4 tablespoons honey
a pinch of salt
220 g oat flakes
2 drops vanilla essence
vegetable butter, flour
and oil to taste

NOTE

When placing
the small biscuits
onto a baking tray, leave
space between them to
avoid sticking
to each other.

Oat biscuits

Easy
1 hour
12

Turn on the oven at 200°C. Mix butter, sugar, honey and salt on the stove. Stir well and add oat flakes and vanilla essence.

Pour the mixture onto a baking tray, greased with oil and let cool. Spread out and cut into square biscuits. Place on a baking tray, greased with butter and powdered with flour. Bake for eight minutes.

Almond twists

Mix the margarine with the flour; stir well. Add sugar, grated almond, anise and vanilla. Knead and shape into a ball; refrigerate for 15 minutes.

Grease an oven tray with vegetable butter and sprinkle with flour. Turn on the oven at 200° C. Powder the work table with flour

and make small rolls with the dough, shaping it into twists.

Place on a baking tray and sprinkle with chopped almond. Place in the oven for 12 minutes. Turn cakes out of mould with a spatula, but only after warm.

INGREDIENTS

190 g vegetable margarine
240 g flour
90 g sugar
90 g grated almond
a pinch of anise
2 drops of vanilla
essence
vegetable butter, flour
and chopped almonds
to taste

Passion fruit iced cream

Easy
35 minutes
6

Soak gelatine sheets in cold water. Open passion fruits and remove pulp; reserve the rinds and add the fructose to the pulp. Boil on low heat for a minute. Remove from heat and add squeezed gelatine sheets. Let cool completely.

Whip cream firmly. Aside, beat egg white and fold into Chantilly. Stir all into the passion fruit cream and place in the freezer until firm, stirring occasionally. Serve the iced cream into the rinds or, if preferred, into well iced cups and decorate with mint leaves.

Strawberry meringues

Turn on the oven at 100°C. Place a sheet of waxed paper on a baking tray, greased with vegetable butter. Beat the egg whites and add the icing sugar, beating until a firm meringue is obtained. Place in a pastry-cook's bag, with a smooth tip; draw closed circles on the waxed paper. Then form small piles over the edges of the circles and place the meringues in the oven for an hour.

Prepare the cream: Put the milk on the stove with the lemon rind. Aside, mix the flour with the sugar and egg yolks. When the milk boils, add the previous mixture. Strain and heat again, stir until thickened.

Let cool. Meanwhile, wash and cut the strawberries; start assembling the dessert: fill cream into the meringues and then add the strawberries. Serve chilled.

INGREDIENTS

4 four egg whites
250 g icing sugar
500 ml milk
1 lemon rind
50 g flour
100 g sugar
5 egg yolks
vegetable butter
and strawberries
to taste

INGREDIENTS

Dough:
2 teaspoons yeast powder
80 g grated or crushed hazelnuts
200 g sugar
1 tablespoon cinnamon
250 ml milk

Cream:
2 tablespoons custard
50 ml light milk
3 tablespoons sugar
1 lemon rind
1 stick cinnamon
vegetable butter
and cinnamon powder
to taste

Easy
30 minutes
4

Hazelnut
and cinnamon puff cake

Mix ingredients for the dough in the order described above, until paste is formed. Grease a round mould with vegetable butter and fill with mixture. Steam for 30 minutes on low heat. Remove and let dry and cool.

Prepare cream: Dissolve custard in a little milk then add the rest. Also add the remaining ingredients and cook on low heat; stir until thickened. After cooling a little, remove cinnamon stick and lemon rind and pour cream over the cake. Decorate with cinnamon powder.

Apple cream

Peel the apples, cut into cubes and sprinkle with lemon juice. Put on stove with yellow sugar on low heat, without dispersing them.

Prepare the cream, stirring the sugar in with the custard. Add the milk, stirring continuously. Place on low heat until thickened; remove and let cool. Arrange alternate layers of apple and cream in cups.

INGREDIENTS

4 reinette apples
3 tablespoons yellow
sugar
4 tablespoons sugar
2 tablespoons custard
powder
1 tablespoon milk
lemon juice to taste

500 ml water
100 ml olive oil
250 g yellow sugar
250 g wheat flour
70 g corn flour
350 g dried figs
cinnamon powder, fennel,
granulated sugar, flour,
corn jam, vegetable
butter and salt to taste

SUGGESTION
Replace the dried figs
with the same quantity
of walnut kernels.

Fig fritters

Easy //
40 minutes
4

Place water, olive oil and yellow sugar on the stove; season with salt, a little cinnamon and fennel. As soon as it begins to boil, add the flours one at a time and stir until thickened. Remove from heat; let cool a little and add dried figs, cut into pieces.

Divide the dough into small portions; shape balls and then flatten them. Mark them with a knife and arrange on a baking tray greased with butter and floured. Brush with corn jam, powder with granulated sugar and place in the oven pre-heated to 200° C, for approximately 15 minutes. Remove still warm fritters from the baking tray and serve.

Chocolate vanilla cake

Turn on the oven at 180° C. Grease two round moulds with Soya butter and line the bases with waxed paper, also greased.

Beat the cocoa with sugar, salt and yeast. Add the oil, water, Soya milk and crushed tofu; beat until a creamy mixture is formed. Add the flour gradually and divide the dough into the moulds. Place in the oven for 35 minutes; turn out of the moulds and leave to cool.

Prepare the cream: Combine two and a half spoonfuls of custard with half of the yellow sugar, lemon rind and half of the butter. Pour in the vanilla milk. Place on low heat until it thickens. Leave to cool, stirring occasionally. Proceed in the same way with the remaining ingredients and prepare the second cream. Cover one of the cakes with the vanilla cream and arrange the other cake on top. Cover it with the chocolate cream and decorate to taste.

INGREDIENTS

30 g cocoa powder
280 g yellow sugar
1 pinch salt
1 teaspoon yeast powder
100 g oil
100 ml water
150 ml Soya milk
120 g tofu
350 g flour
Soya butter to taste

Creams:
3 tablespoons custard
6 tablespoons yellow sugar
1 lemon rind
100 g Soya butter
500 ml vanilla Soya milk
500 ml chocolate Soya milk

30 g baker's yeast
350 ml Soya milk
650 g flour
80 g sugar
80 g vegetable butter
at room temperature
50 g toasted and
crushed almonds

Filling:
4 apples
4 tablespoons sugar
1 teaspoon
cinnamon powder
2 tablespoons
corn jam
2 tablespoons
chopped almond

Apple and almond cake

Easy
1 hour
8

Dissolve the yeast in 150 ml of warm milk. Add 100 grams of flour and knead well. Let rise until the volume is doubled. Add the sugar, butter, almonds and remaining flour. Knead well and leave to rise until the volume is doubled.

Set the oven at 180° C. Roll the dough out, making it very thin. Peel and cut the apples into cubes; sprinkle with sugar and cinnamon and spread over the dough. Roll up and place in the oven for 30 minutes. Remove and brush with corn jam heated with a few drops of water. Sprinkle with chopped almonds.

Banana fritters

Easy
35 minutes
10

Set the oven at 180° C. Crush the banana with a fork and beat with the sugar and eggs. Add the yoghurt, grated bread and yeast. Continue to beat and mix in the grated lemon.

Distribute the preparation into small moulds of ribbed paper. Sprinkle with yellow sugar and place in the oven to cook for 25 minutes. Serve warm or cold.

INGREDIENTS

1 banana
250 g yellow sugar
3 eggs
1 Soya yoghurt
300 g grated bread
1 coffeespoon
yeast powder
1/2 lemon (grated)
yellow sugar to taste

SUGGESTION

Substitute the banana with two cooked carrots, reduced to a purée.

INGREDIENTS

100 g corn jam
8 tinned pear halves
100 ml barley coffee
50 ml orange juice
12 wholemeal biscuits
3 tablespoons custard flour
3 tablespoons fructose
600 ml Soya milk
2 lemon rinds
1 cinnamon stick
100 ml Soya cream

OPTION

Exchange the custard cream for instant pudding. To make it, replace the fructose and the Soya milk with sugar and cow's milk.

Spring cream

Easy

35 minutes

4

Heat the jam; add the pears cut into half moons and leave to gain a caramel colour. Remove the fruit and add the coffee and orange juice to the jam in the pan; leave to boil a little more. Remove from the heat and pour over the biscuits divided into pieces; set aside.

Mix the custard flour with two and a half tablespoons of fructose. Add the milk and place on the stove with the lemon rind and cinnamon stick. Cook until thickened. Leave to cool. Beat the cream with the remaining fructose. Distribute the biscuits, pears and cream into cups in layers. Decorate with cream.

Almond
and pistacchio tart

Grease a dish with vegetable oil and set aside. Set the oven at 180° C. Mix the icing sugar with the butter; add the almonds and pistachios. Finally, add the Soya milk, honey, grated orange, cinnamon and egg; mix well.

Brush the brick dough sheets with water and layer them, one by one, in the dish, so as to cover the base and sides. Fill with the preparation. Fold the dough inside and sprinkle with chopped almond. Place in the oven for 35 minutes. Remove the tart and brush with corn jam.

INGREDIENTS

250 g icing sugar
100 g vegetable butter
200 g ground skinned
almonds
50 g ground pistachios
150 ml Soya milk
1 tablespoon honey
1 orange peel
1 coffeespoon
cinnamon powder
1 egg
6 brick dough sheets
50 g chopped shelled
almonds
2 tablespoons corn jam
vegetable butter
to taste

SUGGESTION
Add to the filler mixture
half a teaspoon of
soluble coffee, when
adding the cinnamon.

200 g vegetable butter
200 g yellow sugar
1 banana
1 tablespoon honey
100 g chocolate powder
250 g flour
1 coffeespoon powdered yeast
1 teaspoon cinnamon
1/2 cup walnut kernels

Topping:
150 g sugar
5 tablespoons water
200 ml coconut milk
150 g walnut kernels

Chocolate and walnut cake

Easy

1 hour

10

Set the oven at 180° C. Grease a 22 cm diameter mould with butter and sprinkle with flour. Beat the butter with the yellow sugar; add the crushed banana, honey and chocolate powder; stir.

Mix the sifted flour with the yeast and cinnamon. Chop the walnut kernels, add to the previous preparation and blend. Pour the mixture into the mould and place in the oven for 45 minutes. Remove and take the cake out of the mould while it is still warm.

Topping: Place the sugar on the stove with the water until it caramelises. Add the coconut milk and let boil a little longer. Add the walnut kernels which have been split in half and mix in delicately. Leave to cool, cover the cake and serve.

Fruit crush

Prepare the pulp: Mix the flour with the starch in a bowl; add the water and blend until a cream is obtained. Set aside.

Make the sauce: Place the sugar in a frying pan and sprinkle with water. Place on the stove until caramel is obtained; add the cream and leave to boil; set aside. Heat the oil on the stove.

Arrange the fruit: Peel the bananas, sprinkle with lemon juice and cut them, like the pineapple, into pieces, then coat them with breadcrumbs. Skewer the fruit pieces, coat with the pulp and fry them; repeat this operation until there is no more fruit. Pour the caramel sauce on top and sprinkle with sesame seeds.

INGREDIENTS

100 g flour
25 g starch
150 ml chilled sparkling
water

Caramel sauce:
200 g yellow sugar
100 ml vegetable cream
sesame seed to taste
2 bananas
1 lemon (juice)
4 pineapple rounds
oil, grated bread
and sesame seeds
to taste

INGREDIENTS

1 tablespoon starch
250 ml Soya milk
500 ml Soya cream
100 g sugar
1 tablespoon
vegetable butter
250 g strawberries
strawberries to taste

Strawberry cream

Easy

35 minutes

4

Dissolve the starch in the milk; add the cream, sugar and butter. Place on low heat, stirring continuously until the blend thickens. Cut the strawberries into pieces and add them to the preparation.

After boiling, remove from the heat and let cool. Distribute into cups. Keep in the fridge and, when serving, decorate with sliced strawberries.

Mango cream

Wash the mangos and peel them; keep a few slices for decoration and reduce the remaining pulp to purée. Place on low heat together with the sugar and water; leave to cook until a thick bright cream is obtained.

Add the agar-agar seaweed and leave to cook for a further five minutes. Distribute into cups and keep in the fridge until it becomes firm. Decorate with the remaining mango.

INGREDIENTS

2 mangos
100 g sugar
100 ml water
1 tablespoon agar-agar
seaweed

SUGGESTION
Add small pieces
of crushed biscuits
to the dessert.

INGREDIENTS

625 g wheat flour
440 g yellow sugar
1 teaspoon cinnamon
    powder
150 g vegetable butter at
    room temperature
125 ml of water
1/2 lemon (grated)
150 g of chopped
    walnut kernels
2 tablespoons corn jam
    flour and vegetable
    butter as needed

Walnut cookies

Easy
30 minutes
10

Mix the flour, sugar, cinnamon and butter; knead and add the water, grated lemon and walnut kernels. After kneading, leave to rest for 15 minutes. Sprinkle the work top with flour; roll the dough out, moulding into small cookies.

Set the oven at 180º C. Distribute the cookies on a baking tray previously greased with vegetable butter. Flatten them and brush with the jam which has been heated in two soupspoons of water. Place in the oven for 10 minutes. Remove and serve.

Caramel delight

Arrange the quinces, removing the skin and seeds. Cut them into pieces and cook in water with the anise and yellow sugar. Drain and distribute into cups; leave to cool.

Beat the cream until it becomes a little thick. Add the lemon juice, white sugar and beat a little longer. Distribute on top of the quince dessert and sprinkle with cinnamon powder.

INGREDIENTS

4 ripe quinces
1 aniseed star
4 tablespoons yellow sugar
250 ml Soya cream
1 tablespoon lemon juice
1 tablespoon white sugar
cinnamon powder to taste

SUGGESTION
Add 80 grams of chopped dried fruit to the quince preparation.

INGREDIENTS

1 tablespoon agar-agar seaweed
550 ml water
300 g tinned pineapple
100 g sugar
1 tablespoon custard powder
200 ml vegetable cream

Pineapple mousse

Easy
40 minutes
4

Dissolve the agar-agar seaweed in 500 ml of water. Put on a low heat with the pineapple and half of the sugar, leaving to cook for five minutes. Dissolve the custard into the remaining water and mix into the previous preparation.

Remove from the heat and leave to cool. Beat the cream with the remaining sugar and fold into the pineapple preparation. Place the mousse in cups and decorate to taste.

Chocolate cake

Easy // 1 hour 6

Grease a round 20 cm cake tin, with vegetable butter and powder with flour. Dissolve the carob bean flour in the water. Mix the lemon juice with the milk separately and leave to rest for a few minutes, until the milk curdles.

Beat the margarine with the sugar separately, until a creamy mixture is obtained. Gradually add the flour and previously sieved yeast. Add the milk mixture and mix in delicately. Add the carob bean, vanilla and mix well.

Pour the mixture into the tin and place in the oven at 180° C, for 40 minutes. Take the cake out of the mould and leave to cool. Split the chocolate into pieces and place on the stove in a bain marie until they melt. Pour the cream over the cake and serve.

INGREDIENTS

80 g carob bean flour
100 ml boiling water
1 tablespoon lemon juice
100 ml Soya milk
100 g vegetable margarine
at room temperature
150 g yellow sugar
250 g flour
1 tablespoon
powdered yeast
3 drops vanilla essence
100 g chocolate bar
vegetable butter
and flour to taste

CHOCOLATE CREAM
Melt 250 ml of milk,
300 grams of chocolate
and 50 grams of
vegetable butter in a bain
marie.

Contents